Ordnance Survey
Road Atlas of Ireland

CONTENTS

I	DISTANCE BETWEEN PRINCIPAL TOWNS
II	ROUTE PLANNER
III	PRINCIPAL TRAFFIC SIGNS REPUBLIC OF IRELAND
IV	PRINCIPAL TRAFFIC SIGNS NORTHERN IRELAND
V	TRAVEL INFORMATION REPUBLIC OF IRELAND
VI	TRAVEL INFORMATION NORTHERN IRELAND
VII	CONVERSION TABLES
VIII	LEGEND TO NATIONAL MAPS
1 - 36	NATIONAL MAPS
37	TOURIST OFFICES
38	INDEX TO TOWN MAPS
39 - 62	TOWN MAPS
63 - 73	TOURING AREAS AND INFORMATION
74 - 86	GAZETTEER
87	GOLFING INFORMATION

INDEX MAP: INSIDE FRONT COVER

Published in 1993 by
Ordnance Survey of Ireland
Phoenix Park, Dublin
and
Ordnance Survey of Northern Ireland
Stranmillis Court, Belfast BT9 5BJ
© Ordnance Survey of Ireland and
Ordnance Survey of Northern Ireland, 1993
Printed by
Ordnance Survey of Ireland Phoenix Park, Dublin.

The distances quoted in the chart below are obtained by using the best available roads and are represented by

Miles in black

Kilometres in red

Kilometres

BELFAST 166 60 227 45 21 513 132 87 417 180 338 138 306 284 436 34 150 323 117 183 87 177 137 61 117 251 224 330 206 346 425 333 309 309

DUBLIN 129 127 195 187 346 114 237 254 233 230 184 212 114 304 204 237 193 232 193 125 87 48 105 174 85 156 153 214 177 298 163 257 135

ARMAGH 158 82 85 468 72 98 383 127 269 87 237 264 389 93 122 278 109 126 27 143 106 31 61 212 156 285 156 307 380 293 253 264

ATHLONE 253 246 311 84 254 219 183 111 142 93 116 232 261 230 121 209 43 129 47 101 163 185 71 32 201 117 137 222 164 150 184

BALLYMENA 68 560 167 43 476 146 362 135 336 309 481 34 122 302 82 220 122 228 183 108 90 280 251 348 200 375 473 357 302 331

BANGOR 534 153 109 438 201 359 159 327 306 457 60 171 344 138 204 108 198 158 82 135 272 245 351 227 367 446 354 330 330

BANTRY 393 566 90 484 225 442 293 243 77 547 533 188 541 354 438 357 394 452 486 302 343 294 428 185 108 214 377 277

CAVAN 171 302 114 195 53 177 175 315 166 156 204 151 53 45 61 68 97 130 84 267 121 225 306 224 188 256

COLERAINE 481 119 391 148 323 346 488 76 82 378 50 224 126 232 204 129 105 301 254 391 185 230 479 394 288 372

CORK 402 137 360 209 148 87 451 449 105 428 262 348 245 275 351 404 175 251 208 336 103 119 126 293 187

DONEGAL 272 61 204 309 407 228 48 296 69 146 121 190 182 158 68 254 151 391 66 320 397 357 169 372

ENNIS 245 67 150 145 372 322 37 343 154 240 158 203 278 288 151 125 245 203 79 138 166 150 227

ENNISKILLEN 183 232 364 172 101 262 98 85 60 114 121 111 43 183 119 312 68 278 364 280 171 294

GALWAY 172 193 330 251 104 272 111 222 140 169 264 227 151 80 274 138 145 206 220 83 253

KILKENNY 198 319 333 113 335 156 220 118 146 219 275 51 158 98 245 76 214 48 256 80

KILLARNEY 470 455 111 441 275 360 278 323 402 407 225 264 275 343 132 32 193 277 254

LARNE 146 357 114 217 120 211 171 95 119 285 249 364 240 380 459 367 343 346

LETTERKENNY 351 32 187 113 217 188 153 60 286 198 391 113 367 452 381 215 372

LIMERICK 328 164 249 150 195 265 306 114 149 211 232 40 101 129 179 190

LONDONDERRY 183 108 212 201 140 55 282 211 397 135 346 430 383 238 378

LONGFORD 90 43 88 140 129 113 31 242 106 180 265 204 146 224

MONAGHAN 106 93 51 53 175 129 280 126 270 351 269 225 261

MULLINGAR 45 116 158 69 64 198 135 166 251 164 179 180

NAVAN 76 146 100 109 203 188 191 296 195 224 183

NEWRY 93 190 171 259 177 285 367 267 275 240

OMAGH 227 163 333 111 322 407 322 214 314

PORTLAOISE 103 135 188 95 216 100 200 116

ROSCOMMON 241 85 169 251 208 114 222

ROSSLARE 327 124 291 79 352 19

SLIGO 254 335 293 103 307

TIPPERARY 111 82 220 143

TRALEE 212 282 272

WATERFORD 309 61

WESTPORT 333

WEXFORD

103
37 80
141 79 98
28 121 51 157
13 116 53 153 42
319 215 291 193 348 332
82 71 45 52 104 95 244
54 147 61 158 27 68 352 106
259 158 238 136 296 272 56 188 299
112 145 79 114 91 125 301 71 74 250
210 143 167 69 225 223 140 121 243 85 169
86 109 54 88 84 99 275 33 92 224 38 152
190 132 147 58 209 203 182 110 201 130 127 42 114
177 71 164 72 192 190 151 109 215 92 192 93 144 107
271 189 242 144 299 284 48 196 303 54 253 90 226 120 123
21 127 58 162 21 37 340 103 47 280 142 231 107 205 198 292
93 147 76 143 76 106 331 97 51 279 30 200 63 156 207 283 91
201 120 173 75 231 214 117 127 235 65 184 23 163 65 70 69 222 218
73 144 68 130 51 86 336 94 31 266 43 213 61 169 208 274 71 20 204
114 79 78 27 137 127 220 33 139 163 91 96 53 69 97 171 135 116 102 114
54 78 17 80 76 67 272 28 78 216 75 149 37 138 137 224 75 70 155 67 56
110 54 89 29 142 123 122 38 144 152 118 98 71 87 73 173 131 135 93 132 27 66
85 30 66 63 114 98 245 42 127 171 113 126 75 105 91 201 106 117 121 125 55 58 28
38 65 19 101 67 51 281 54 80 218 98 173 69 164 136 250 59 95 165 87 32 72 47
73 108 38 115 56 84 302 60 65 251 42 179 27 141 171 253 74 37 190 34 80 33 98 91 58
156 53 132 44 174 169 188 81 187 109 158 94 114 94 32 140 177 178 71 175 70 109 43 62 118 141
139 97 97 20 156 152 213 52 158 156 94 78 74 50 98 164 155 123 93 131 19 80 40 68 106 101 64
205 95 177 125 216 218 183 166 243 129 243 152 194 170 61 171 226 243 131 247 150 174 123 126 161 207 150
128 133 93 73 124 141 266 75 115 209 41 128 42 86 152 213 149 70 145 84 66 78 84 117 110 69 117 53 203
215 110 191 85 233 228 115 140 143 64 199 49 173 90 47 82 236 228 25 215 112 168 103 119 177 200 59 105 77 158
264 185 236 138 294 277 68 190 298 74 247 86 226 128 133 20 285 281 63 267 165 218 156 184 228 253 134 156 181 208 69
207 101 185 102 222 220 134 139 245 78 222 103 174 31 120 228 237 80 238 127 167 102 121 166 200 62 129 49 182 51 132
192 160 157 93 188 205 234 117 179 182 105 94 106 52 159 172 215 134 112 148 91 140 111 139 171 133 137 71 219 64 137 175 192
192 84 164 114 205 205 172 159 231 116 231 141 183 157 50 158 215 231 118 235 139 162 112 114 149 195 72 138 12 191 89 169 38 207

Miles

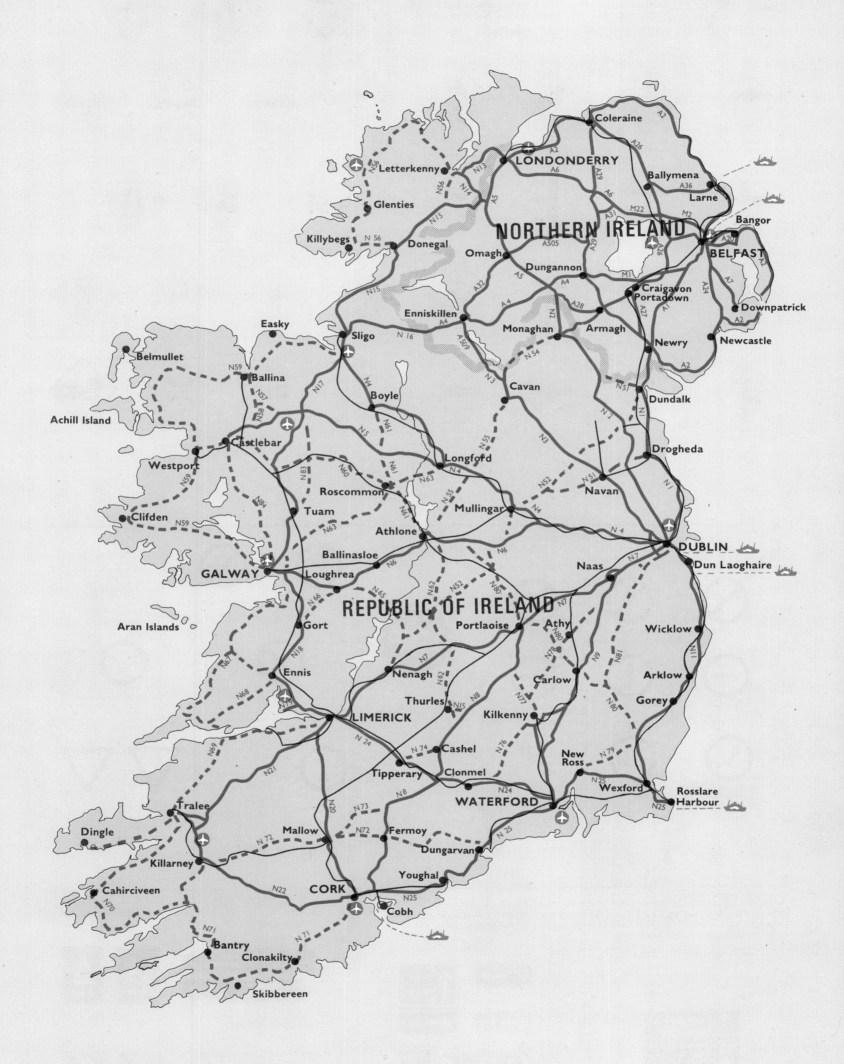

PRINCIPAL TRAFFIC SIGNS - REPUBLIC OF IRELAND

WARNING SIGNS give advance warning of a hazard and are in black on a yellow background. The following are examples of the principal warning signs.

Roundabout Ahead

End of Dual Carriageway

Two-Way Traffic

Dangerous Corner Ahead

Dangerous Bend Ahead

Series of Dangerous Corners Ahead

Series of Dangerous Bends Ahead

Slippery Stretch of Road Ahead

Sharp Rise Ahead e.g. Hump-Back Bridge

Sharp Depression Ahead

Series of Bumps or Hollows Ahead

Junction Ahead with road or roads of *equal importance*

Steep Ascent Ahead

Steep Descent Ahead

Road Narrows Dangerously Ahead or Narrow Bridge Ahead

Junction Ahead with roads of *less importance* (minor road(s) shown by thin arms)

Unprotected Quay, Canal or River Ahead

Road Works Ahead

Children Sign (School, etc.)

Traffic Lights Ahead

Staggered Junction Ahead
with roads of equal importance

with roads of less importance

Advance Warning (where vision is limited) of a major road ahead marked by a "Stop" sign or "Yield Right of Way" sign.

Low Bridge Ahead

Level Crossing Ahead guarded by gates or lifting barriers

Level Crossing Ahead, unguarded by gates or lifting barriers

Level Crossing Ahead with Lights and barriers

REGULATORY SIGNS implement road regulations and show the course to follow etc. The colour red is used. The following are examples of the principal signs:

No Left Turn

No Entry

No Right Turn

Traffic may *not* proceed in direction of arrow

Turn Left

Straight Ahead Only

Turn Right

Traffic may proceed *only* in direction of arrow

Keep to Left Carriageway (on dual carriageway)

Speed Limit

End of Speed Limit

Parking Permitted

Parking Prohibited

Note: periods etc. for which parking is permitted or prohibited may be shown on a plaque placed beneath the sign. Arrows indicating the direction in which parking is permitted or prohibited may be shown on the sign

STOP
Stop Sign

Stop before entering the major road ahead and give way to traffic on it

Clearway — stopping or parking prohibited (except by buses or taxis) for the periods indicated on a plaque placed beneath the sign

To indicate an appointed Taxi Stand. Other vehicles must not park here

School Warden's Sign
Approaching traffic must stop as long as this sign is exhibited by a school warden assisting school children across the road.

YIELD RIGHT OF WAY   GEILL SLÍ
Major Road Ahead — give way to traffic on it

INFORMATION SIGNS give information regarding direction, distance, place, etc. Signs may be in black lettering on a white background. Newer signs are in white and yellow lettering on a green background. The following are some examples:

LEATAOBH LAY-BY ½ M
Traffic Lay-By Ahead

LEATAOBH LAY-BY
Traffic Lay-By

CUL DE SAC
No Through Road

N11 →
← N11
Loch Garman N11 WEXFORD
← Bré BRAY
Advance Direction Sign

↑ N4 / N7
← N81
< 2 Bré BRAY
An Nás NAAS
Direction Signs

INFORMATION SIGNS
In addition signs of the following kind may be seen to indicate facilities/amenities of particular interest to tourists.

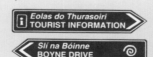
Eolas do Thurasoiri TOURIST INFORMATION →
← Slí na Bóinne BOYNE DRIVE

4 km

2 km

MOTORWAY SIGNS

Motorway ahead
NO L-drivers
Vehicles under 50 c.c.
Slow vehicles (under 30 mph)
Invalid-carriages
Pedal-cycles
Pedestrians
Animals
Motorway Ahead

M1
Entry to Motorway

500m
Approaching end of motorway

Motorway Regulations no longer apply

---

for further information see current Rules of the Road for the Republic of Ireland

PRINCIPAL TRAFFIC SIGNS - NORTHERN IRELAND

SIGNS GIVING ORDERS

These signs are mostly circular and those with red circles are mostly prohibitive

 40 Maximum speed

 National speed limit applies

 STOP — Stop and Give Way

 GIVE WAY — Give way to traffic on major road

 STOP CHILDREN — School crossing patrol

 STOP POLICE

 No entry for vehicular traffic

 No right turn

No left turn

No U turns

No overtaking

No vehicles

No stopping (Clearway)

Give priority to vehicles from opposite direction

URBAN CLEARWAY Monday to Friday am 8-9.30 pm 4.30-6.30 — No stopping during times shown except for up to 2 mins. to set down or pick up passengers

Signs with blue circles but no red border are mostly compulsory

Ahead only

Turn left ahead (right if symbol reversed)

Turn left (right if symbol reversed)

Keep left (right if symbol reversed)

Vehicles may pass either side to reach same destination

Route to be used by pedal cyclists only

30 Minimum speed

End of minimum speed

Mini-roundabout (roundabout circulation – give way to vehicles from the immediate right)

One-way traffic (Note compare circular "Ahead only" sign)

DIRECTION SIGNS

Mostly rectangular

Signs on motorways *Blue backgrounds*

 M1 — Start of motorway

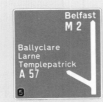 Belfast M2 / Ballyclare Larne Templepatrick A 57 / 5 — On approaches to junctions (junction number on black background)

 M2 Belfast 14 (Larne 17) — Route confirmatory sign after junction

 End of motorway

 Belfast M1 — At the junction

 Carrickfergus Greencastle / Belfast / M2 — Downward pointing arrows mean "Get in lane"

Signs on primary routes *Green backgrounds*

Lurgan Centre Brownlow Craigavon Centre / Gilford B 3 / Banbridge (A 26) — On approaches to junctions

A 1 Belfast 24 Dromore 7 Lisburn 16 — Route confirmatory sign after junction

(A 46) — Route confirmatory sign after junction

 The West Dublin M1 / Shaftesbury Square City Hospital / The Falls / Royal Victoria Hospital — On approaches to junctions (The blue panel indicates that the motorway commences from the junction ahead. The motorway shown in brackets can also be reached by proceeding in that direction)

Banbridge Newry A 1 — At the junction

Signs on non-primary routes *Black borders*

Banbridge A 26 / Lurgan A 26 — On approaches to junctions

R — Ring road

Lurgan A 26 — At the junction

Local direction signs *Blue borders*

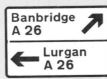 Lurgan A 76 / Annesborough / Craigavon Centre Brownlow (A 3) — On approaches to junctions

Ashfield 2½ — At the junction

 Craigavon Centre Brownlow Portadown / Lough Neagh — On approaches to junctions

WARNING SIGNS

STOP 100 yds — Distance to "Stop" line ahead

Cross roads

Roundabout

T junction

Staggered junction

GIVE WAY 50 yds — Distance to "Give Way" line ahead

Side road

REDUCE SPEED NOW — Plate below some signs

 Sharp deviation of route to left (or right if chevrons reversed)

Bend to right (or left if symbol reversed)

Double bend first to left (may be reversed)

Slippery road

Two-way traffic straight ahead

Two-way traffic crosses one-way road

Traffic merges from left

Traffic merges from right

Road narrows on right (left if symbol reversed)

Road narrows on both sides

Dual carriageway ends

10% — Steep hill downwards

20% — Steep hill upwards — Gradients may be shown as a ratio i.e. 20% = 1:5

School — Children going to or from school

Single file traffic — Single file in each direction

Hump bridge

Uneven road

Traffic signals

Pedestrian crossing

Patrol — School crossing patrol ahead (Some signs have amber lights which flash when patrol is operating)

Single track road — Road wide enough for only one line of traffic

Road works

Change to opposite carriageway (may be reversed)

Right-hand lane closed (symbols may be varied)

Loose chippings

Ford — Worded warning sign

AUTOMATIC BARRIERS STOP when lights show — Plate to indicate a level crossing equipped with automatic barriers and flashing lights

Level crossing with barrier or gate ahead

Level crossing without barrier or gate ahead

Location of level crossing without barrier or gate

 "Count-down" markers approaching concealed level crossing (each bar represents ⅓ the distance from the first warning sign to the crossing)

14'-6" — Height limit (e.g. low bridge)

14'-6" — Available width of headroom indicated

Opening or swing bridge ahead

Quayside or river bank

INFORMATION SIGNS

All rectangular

ONE WAY — One-way street

Priority over vehicles from opposite direction

T — No through road

H — Hospital ahead

P — Parking place; plate may indicate any restrictions on use

P Permit holders only — Parking restricted to use by people named on sign

 Forton Services — Direction to service area with fuel, parking, cafeteria and restaurant facilities

 Appropriate traffic lanes at junction ahead

 "Count-down" markers at exit from motorway (each bar represents 100 yards to the exit) Green-backed markers may be used on primary routes

Other direction signs

Mount Stewart — National Trust Property

300yds — Direction to camping and caravan site

Zoo — Tourist attraction

300yds — Picnic site

for further information see current Highway Code for Northern Ireland

TRAVEL INFORMATION REPUBLIC OF IRELAND

DRIVING IS ON THE LEFT THROUGHOUT IRELAND

SAFETY BELTS must be worn by drivers and passengers

CRASH HELMETS must be worn by motor cyclists and pillion passengers

SPEED LIMITS

The national speed limit is 60 mph/96 kph, but lower limits may apply in towns, in built-up areas and in other roads where so indicated. The limit on motorways is 70 mph/112 kph.

OTHER LIMITS	MPH	KPH
Single deck buses (more than 8 passengers)	50	80
Double deck buses	40	64
Goods vehicles (over 3500KG.)	50	80
Articulated vehicles (without trailer)	50	80
Vehicle drawing one trailer	50	80

for further information see current Rules of the Road for the Republic of Ireland

EMERGENCIES

For Police, Ambulance, Fire Brigade, Life Boat and Coastal Rescue, dial 999 on all automatic telephones, or call Operator on all other telephones.

WEATHER INFORMATION

Phone

Munster	1550 123 850
Leinster	1550 123 851
Connaught	1550 123 852
Ulster	1550 123 853
Dublin	1550 123 854

Sea Area Forecast and Gale Warnings
1550 123 855

ROAD INFORMATION

Automobile Association
Free phone 1 800 667788

PASSENGER SERVICES

BUS

Bus Átha Cliath - Dublin Bus	(01) 8734222
Bus Eireann - Irish Bus	(01) 366111
ATHLONE	(0902) 72651
BALLINA	(096) 21657
BALLYSHANNON	(072) 51101
CASHEL	(062) 52121
CAVAN	(049) 31353
CLONMEL	(052) 22622
CORK	(021) 508188
DROGHEDA	(041) 35023
DUBLIN	(01) 366111
DUNDALK	(042) 34075
ENNIS	(065) 24177
GALWAY	(091) 62000
KILKENNY	(056) 64933
KILLARNEY	(064) 34777
LETTERKENNY	(074) 21309
LIMERICK	(061) 313333
LONGFORD	(043) 45208
MONAGHAN	(047) 82377
ROSSLARE HBR	(053) 33114
SLIGO	(071) 60066
STRANORLAR	(074) 31089
	(074) 31008
TIPPERARY	(062) 51555
TRALEE	(066) 23566
WATERFORD	(051) 790000
WESTPORT	(098) 25711

AIR

Arrivals and departures enquiries (same day only)

Dublin Airport   (01) 7056705

Cork Airport
(0715-2300 hours) (021) 318131
(2300-0700 hours) (021) 965414
Shannon Airport (061) 471444
and (061) 61666

SEA

B&I Car Ferries	Dublin	(01) 6797977
	Cork	(021) 273024
	Rosslare	(053) 33311
Stena Sealink	Dublin	(01) 2807777
	Dunlaoghaire	(01) 2808844
	Rosslare	(053) 33115
	Cork	(021) 272965
	Limerick	(061) 316259
Irish Ferries		
	Dublin	(01) 6610511
	Rosslare	(053) 33158
	Cork	(021) 504333

Brittany Ferries Cork (021) 277801

Swansea / Cork Ferries Cork (021) 271166

RAIL

Iarnrod Eireann,   (01) 366222
Irish Rail
including Dart Suburban Rail Bus

RADIO BROADCASTS
National and local weather and road information are broadcast frequently on the following wavelengths.

RTE	FREQUENCY	INDEPENDENT RADIO		STATION NAME	FREQUENCY	STATION NAME	FREQUENCY
		STATION NAME	FREQUENCY				
RADIO 1	FM 88.1-90.2	**FM 104**	104.4	**RADIO KILKENNY**	96.6	**CKR**	97.3
	kHz M	**DUBLIN**		KILKENNY		CARLOW	97.6
	567 529	**98 FM**	98.1	**RADIO KERRY**	97.0	**TIPP FM**	97.1
CORK LOCAL	729 412	**DUBLIN**		CO KERRY	96.2	CO TIPPERARY	103.9
					97.6		
2FM	FM 90.3-92.4	**CLARE FM**	96.4		95.2	**TIPPERARY MID WEST**	104.8
	kHz M	CO CLARE	95.5			TIPPERARY	
	612 490	**GALWAY BAY FM**	95.8	**NORTH WEST RADIO**	102.5	**RADIO 3**	103.5
DUBLIN AND			96.8	SLIGO	96.3	CO OFFALY	
CORK INCLUDING			97.4				
CORK LOCAL	1278 235			**RADIO LIMERICK 95FM**	95.0	**SHANNONSIDE 104FM**	104.1
FM3 AND		**RADIO LM/FM**	104.9			ROSCOMMON	95.7
RADIO NA		CO LOUTH	95.8	**EAST COAST RADIO**	94.9		
GAELTACHTA	FM 92.6-94.6	Clermont Carn FM3	102.7	CO WICKLOW	102.9	**HIGHLAND RADIO**	103.3
RADIO NA		**MID WEST RADIO**	96.1		96.2	CO DONEGAL	95.2
GAELTACHTA	kHz M	CO MAYO	97.1		104.4		94.7
Connemara	540 556		97.3	**WLR FM**	95.1	**NORTHERN SOUND**	94.8
Donegal	963 312		95.4	WATERFORD	97.5	MONAGHAN	95.3
Kerry	828 362	**COUNTY SOUND/**	96.4				97.5
ATLANTIC 252	kHz M	**96FM**	103.7	**SOUTH EAST RADIO**	99.2		103.4
	252 1190	CO CORK	103.3	WEXFORD	96.2		

RTE HAS IMPLEMENTED AN AUTOMATIC TUNING SYSTEM RDS ON ITS 3 NATIONAL FM NETWORKS
AN RDS RECEIVER CONTINUALLY SCANS FOR THE BEST SIGNAL GIVING OPTIMUM RECEPTION AT ALL TIMES

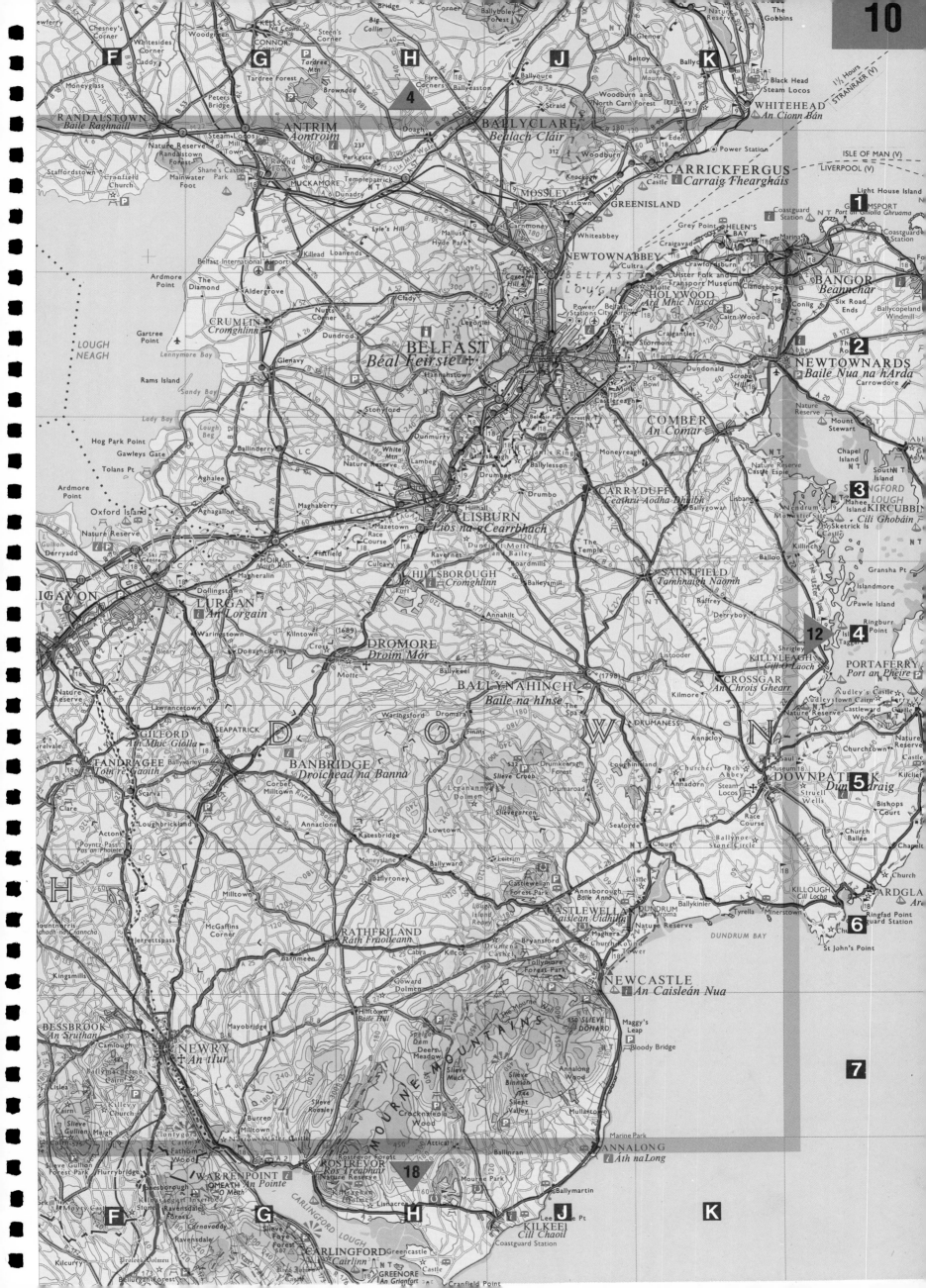

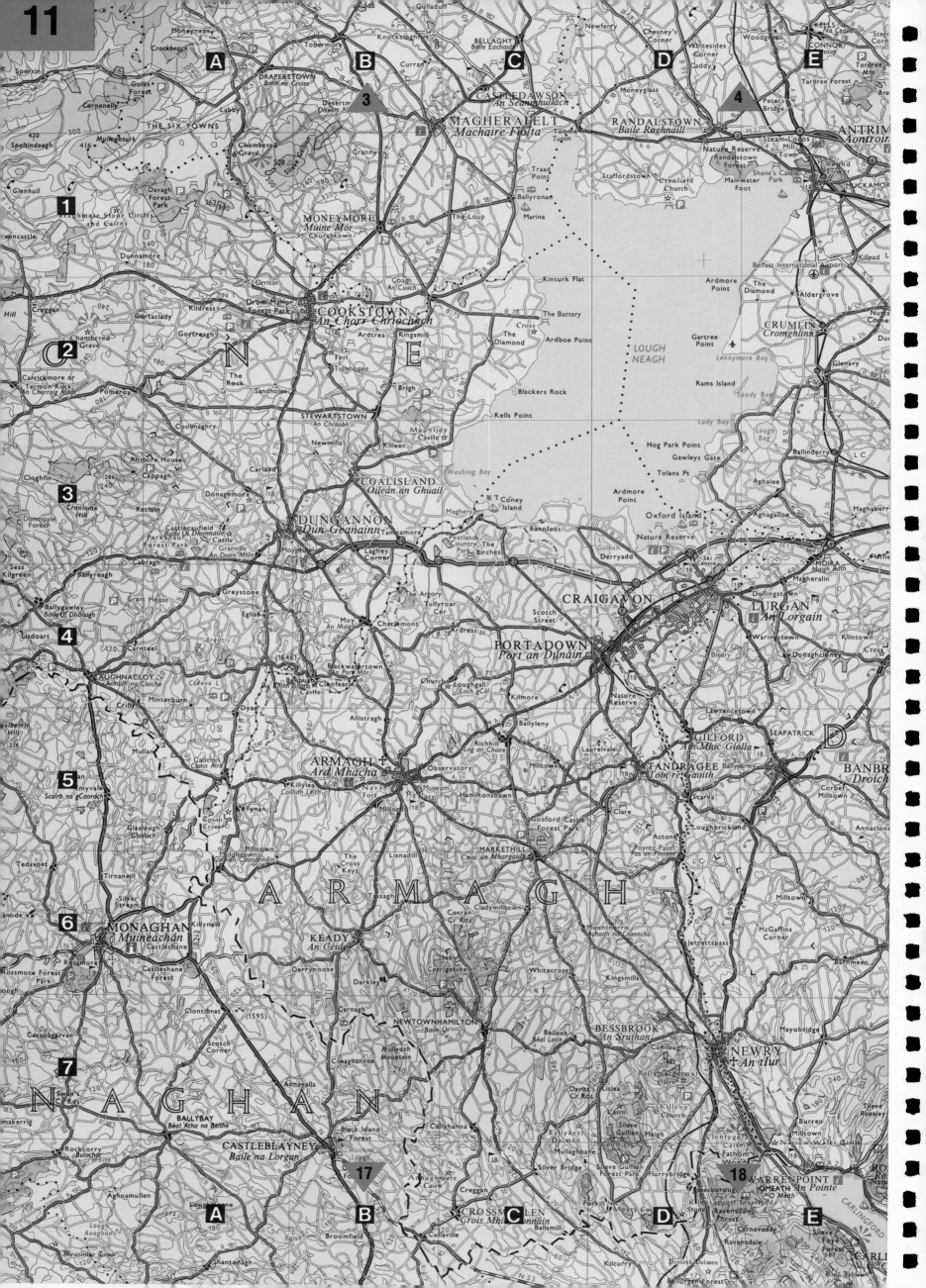

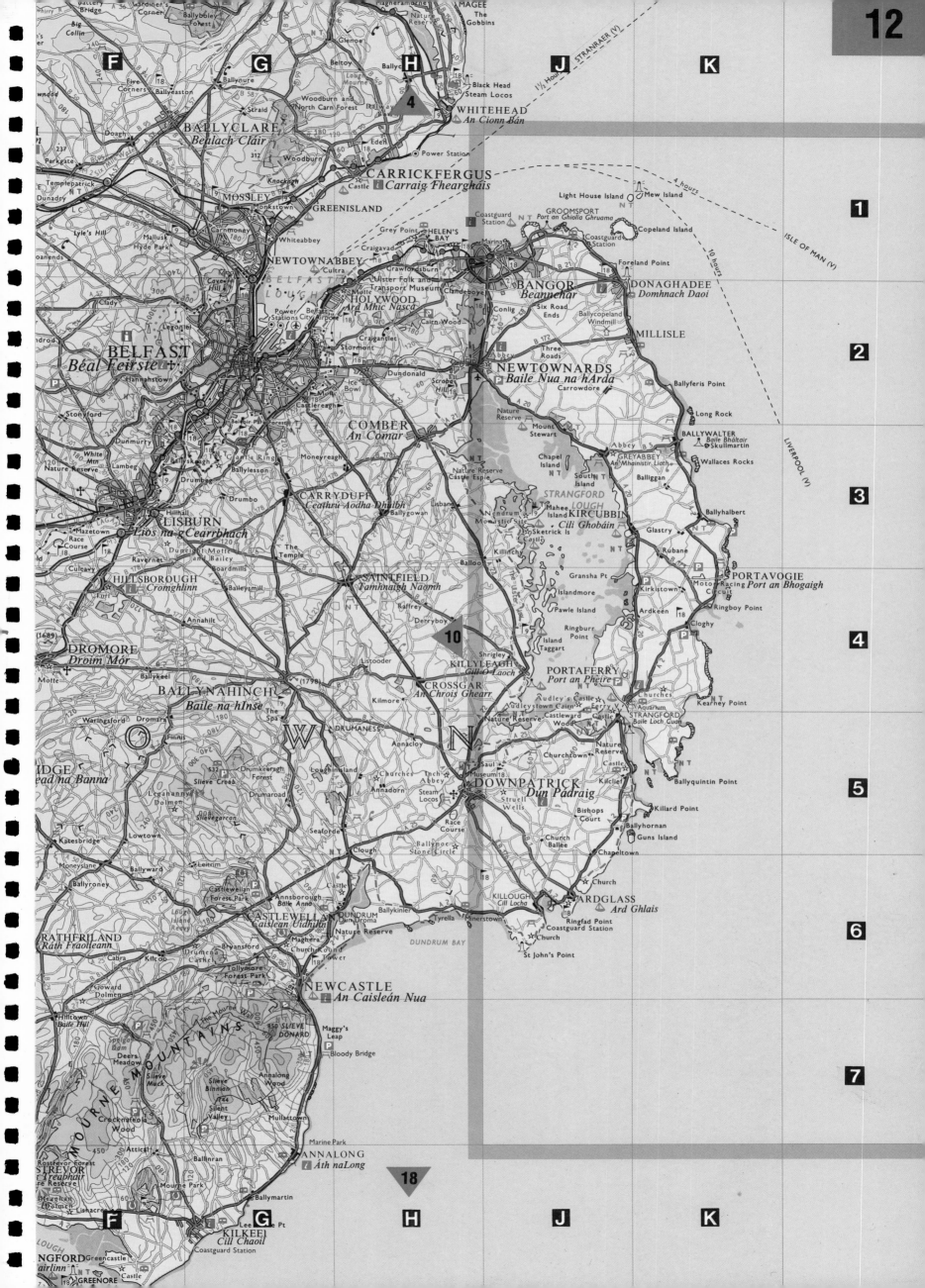

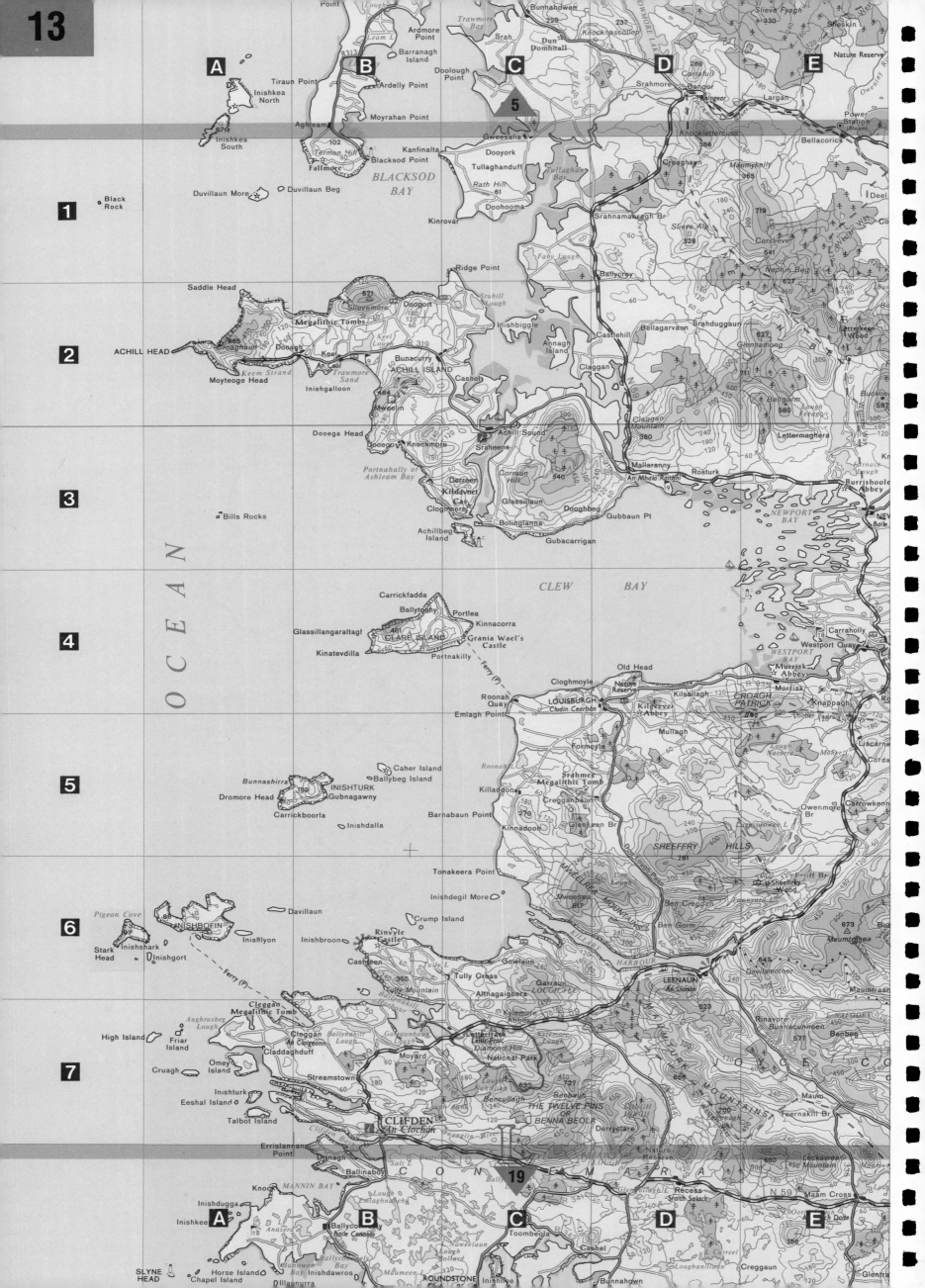

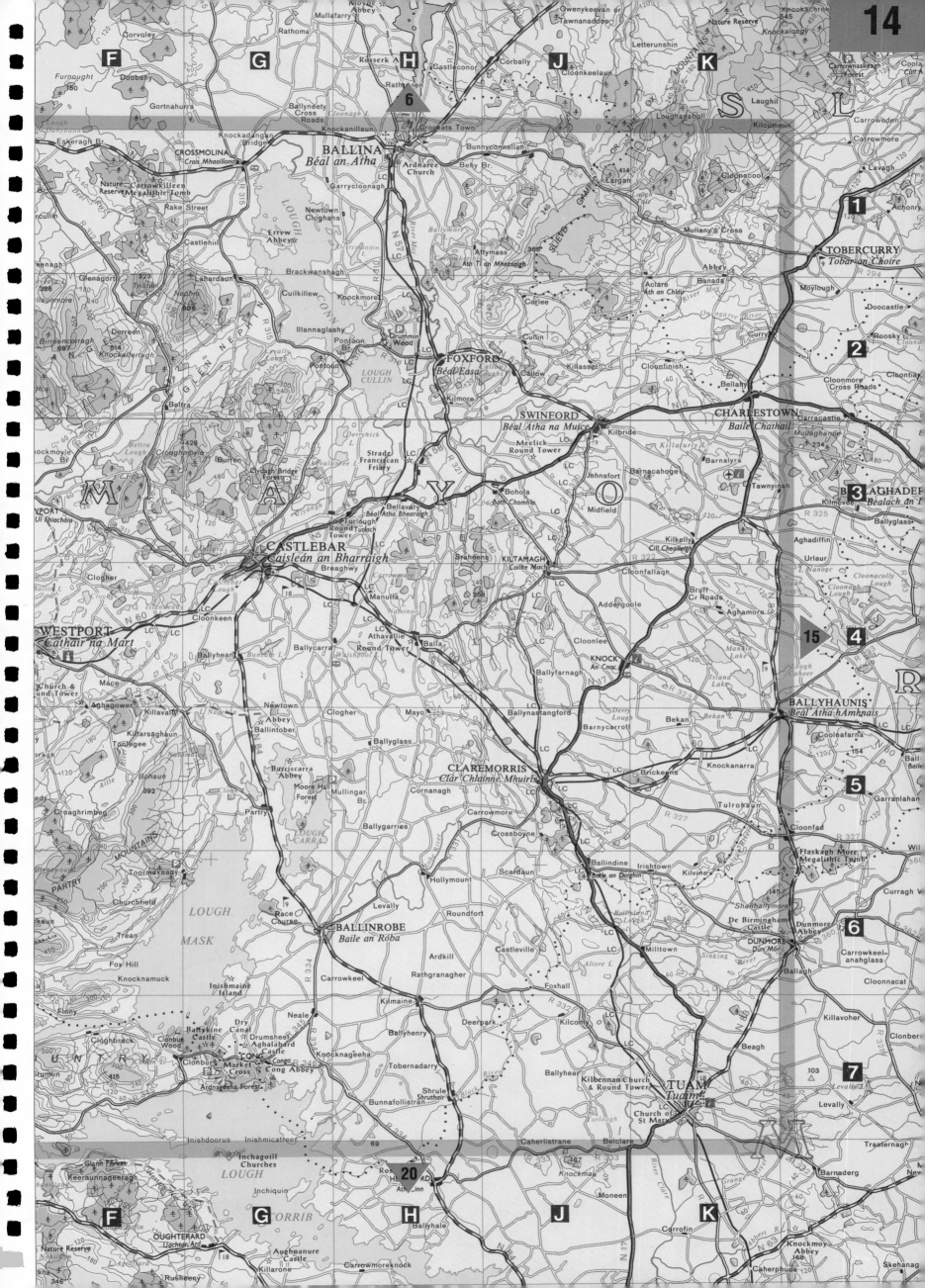

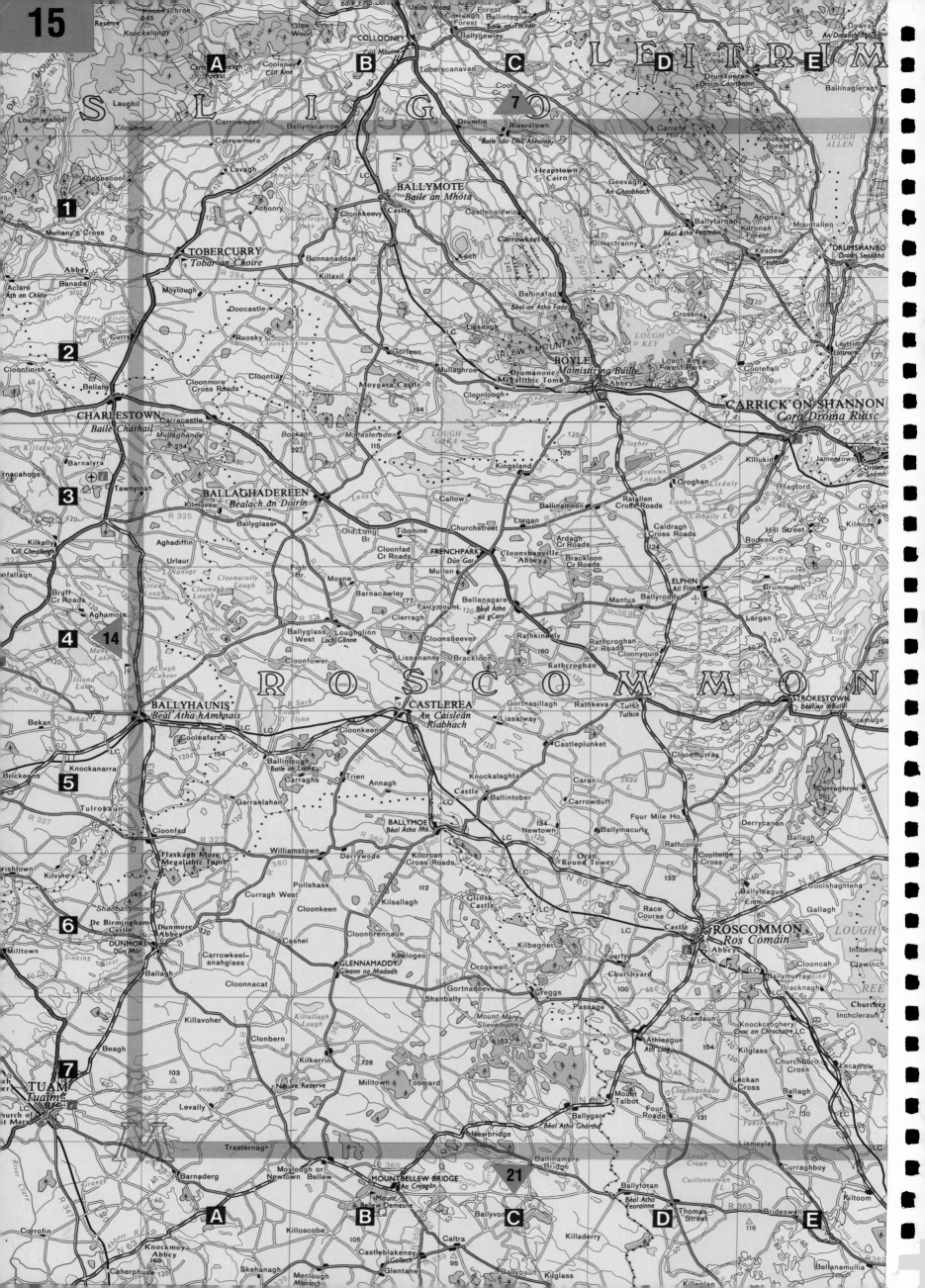

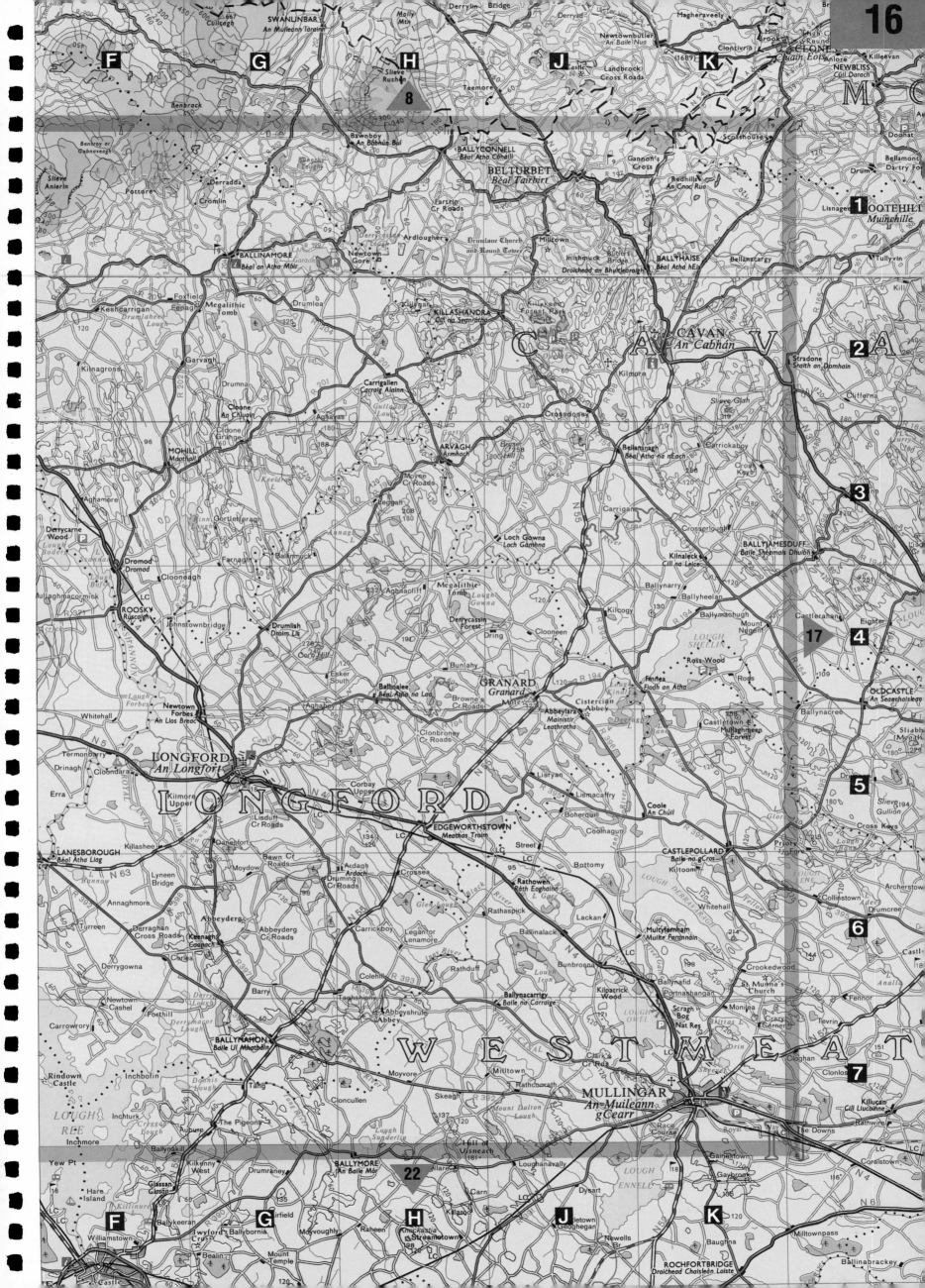

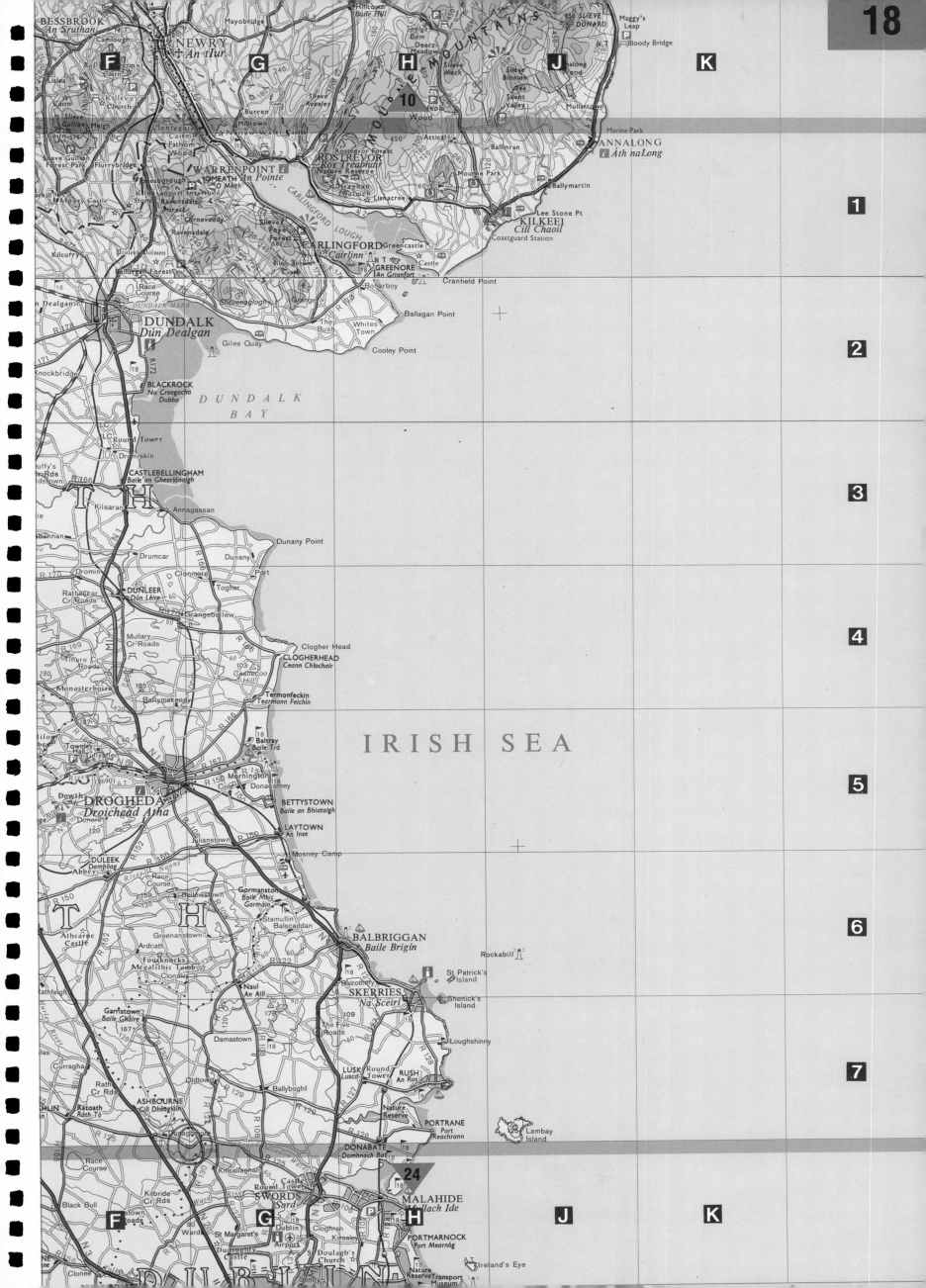

F G H J K

BESSBROOK
An Sruthán
Camlough
NEWRY
An tIúr
Lislea
Killevy
Church
Cairn
Slieve
Gullion
Meigh
Slieve Gullion
Forest Park
Cairn 575
Clontygora Cairn
Flurrybridge
Kilcurry
Bellurgan Forest
Mayobridge
Burren
Milltown
Narrow Water Castle
Fathom
Wood
WARRENPOINT
OMEATH An Pointe
O Meith
Kilbroney
Ravensdale
Carnavaddy
Ravensdale
Race
Course
Shievenaglogh
Grange
Proleek
Dolmen
CARLINGFORD
Cairlinn
Slieve
Foye
587
Spelga
Dam
Deers
Meadow
Slieve
Muck
Speola
Wood
ROSTREVOR
Ros Treabhair
Rostrevor Forest
Nature Reserve
Kilkeeragh
Holme
Lisnacree
Attical
Mourne Park
Ballinran
CARLINGFORD LOUGH
Greencastle
Castle
GREENORE
An Grianfort
Boharboy
Crantield Point
MOURNE MOUNTAINS
SLIEVE
DONARD
Maggy's
Leap
Bloody Bridge
ANNALONG
Áth na Long
Ballymartin
Lee Stone Pt
KILKEEL
Cill Chaoil
Coastguard Station
Slieve
Binnian
744
Silent
Valley
Mullartown
Marine Park

10

24

K 1

Knockbridge
DUNDALK
Dún Dealgan
DUNDALK HARB
BLACKROCK
Na Creagacha
Dubha
Duffy's
Crds
LC
LC Round Tower
Dromiskin
CASTLEBELLINGHAM
Baile an Ghearlánaigh
Kilsaran
Annagassan
Drumcar
Dromin
Rathescar
Cr Roads
DUNLEER
Dún Léire
Grangebellew
Mullary
Cr Roads
Tinure Cr
Roads
Monasterboice
Ballymakenny
Drogheda
Dowth
DROGHEDA
Droichead Átha
Townley
Hall
Lullaren
Mornington
Donacarney
Colp
DULEEK
Damhliag
Abbey
Race
Course
BETTYSTOWN
Baile an Bhiataigh
LAYTOWN
An Inse
Julianstown
Mosney Camp
Giles Quay
The Bush
Whites
Town
Cooley Point
Ballagan Point

DUNDALK
BAY

Dunany Point
Dunany
Port
Togher
Clonmore
Cionmore
Clogher Head
CLOGHERHEAD
Ceann Chlochair
Castlecoo
Hill
103
185
Termonfeckin
Tearmann Feichín
Baltray
Baile Trá

IRISH SEA

Athcarne
Castle
Gormanston
Baile Mhic
Gormáin
Stamullin
Balscaddan
Greenanstown
Ardcath
Fourknocks
Megalithic Tomb
Clonalvy
BALBRIGGAN
Baile Brigín
Rockabill
Balrothery
SKERRIES
Na Sceirí
St Patrick's
Island
Shenick's
Island
The Five
Roads
Loughshinny
Garristown
Baile Ghairie
167
Damastown
LUSK Round
Lusca Tower
RUSH
An Ros
Curragha
Rathfeigh
Rathoath
Cr Rds
Oldtown
Ballyboghil
Naul
An Aill
Nature
Reserve
PORTRANE
Port
Reachrann
Lambay
Island
ASHBOURNE
Cill Dhéagláin
Ratoath
Ráth Tó
Donaghmore
DONABATE
Domhnach Bat
Race
Course
Black Bull
Kilbride
Cr Rds
Kilsallaghan
Castle
Round Tower
SWORDS
Sord
Cloghran
Dublin
Airport
St Margaret's
Ward
St Doulagh's
Church
MALAHIDE
Mullach Íde
PORTMARNOCK
Port Mearnóg
Ireland's Eye
Nature
Reserve Transport
Museum
Clonee
DUBLIN

F G H J K

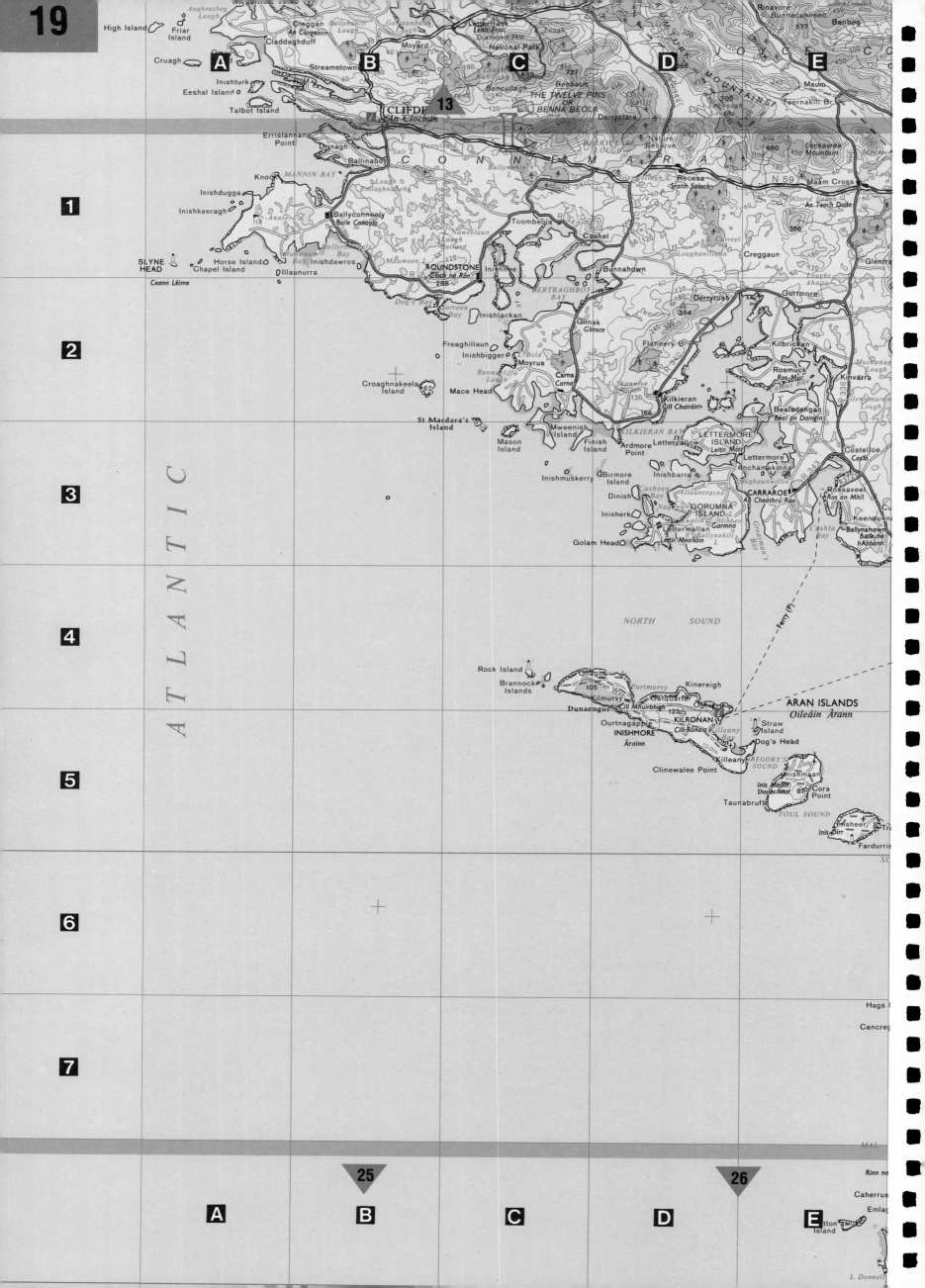

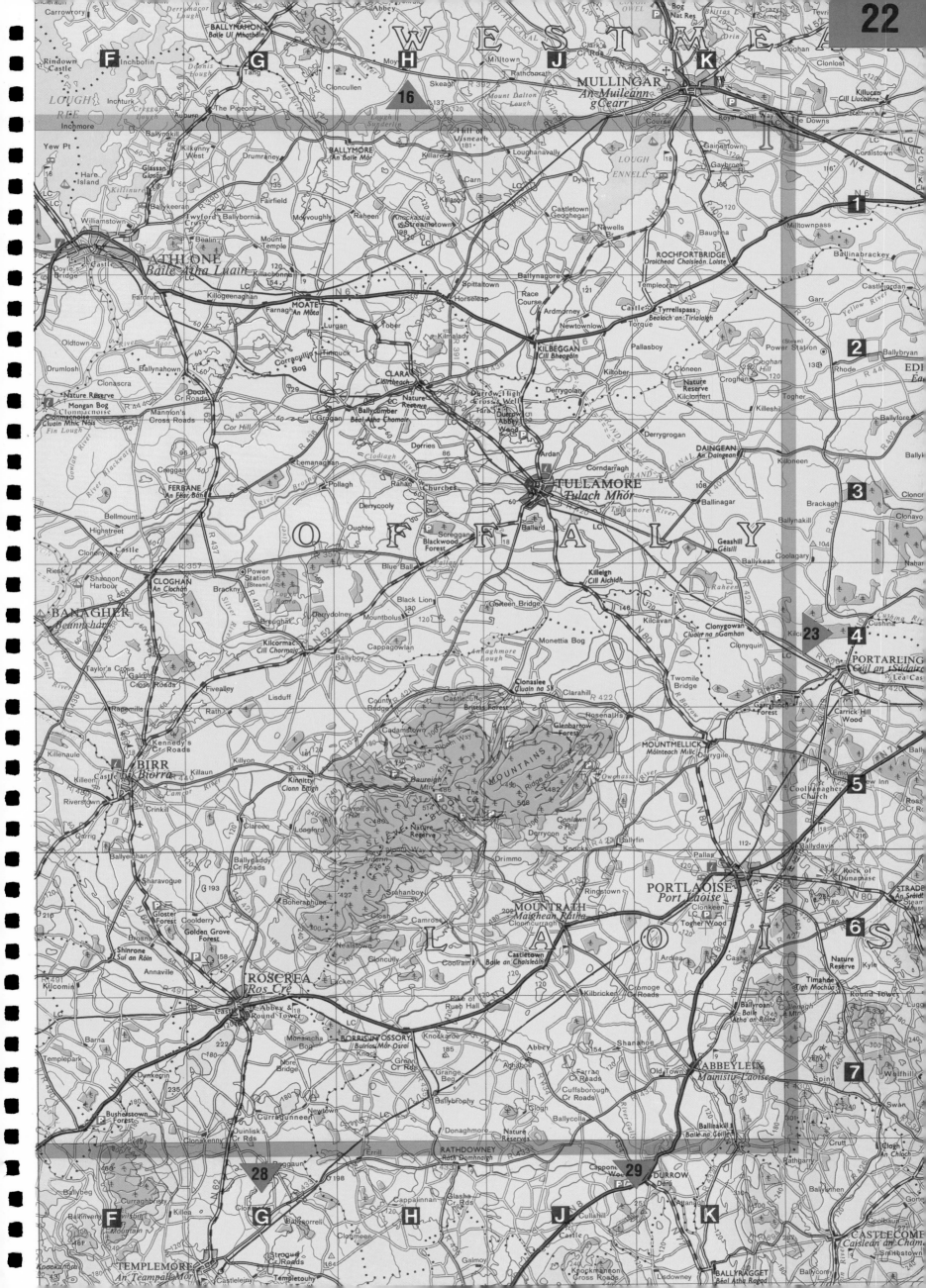

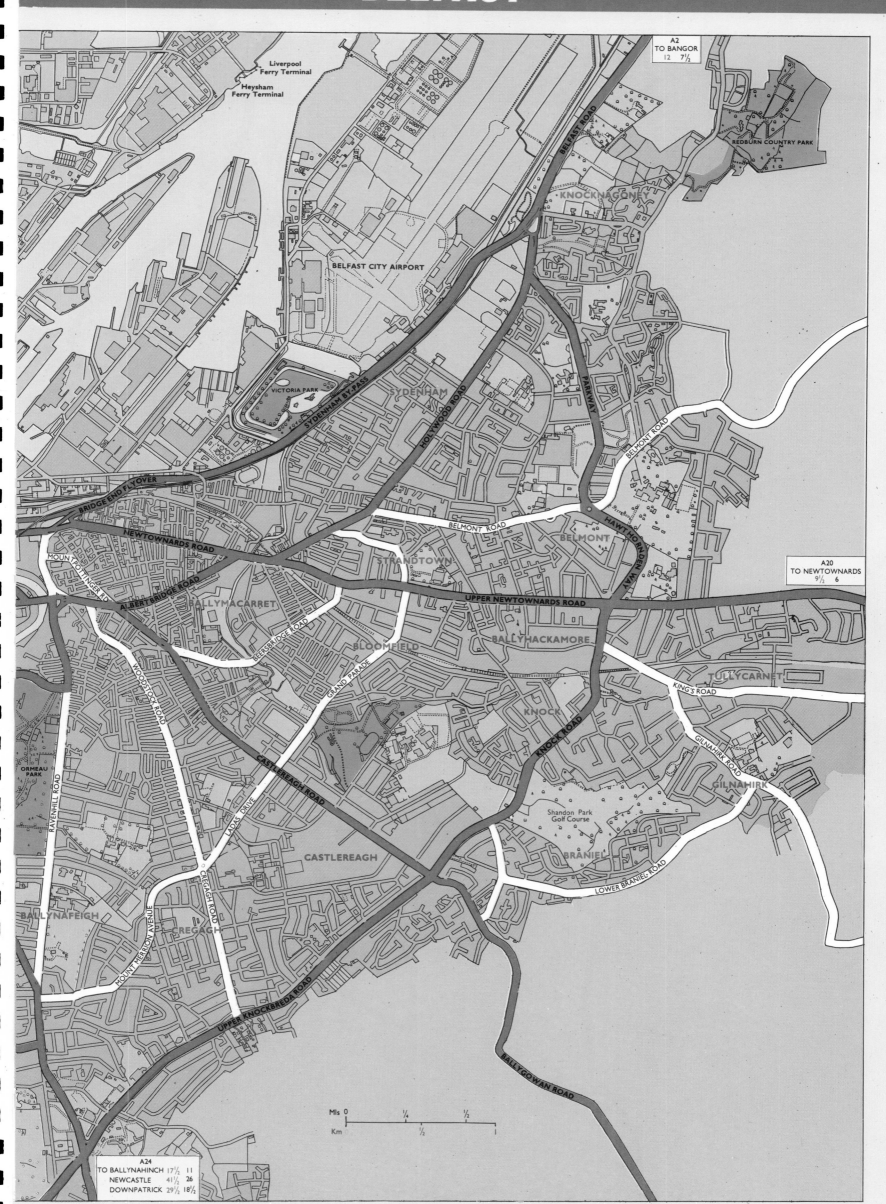

Liverpool
Ferry Terminal

Heysham
Ferry Terminal

A2
TO BANGOR
12 7½

REDBURN COUNTRY PARK

KNOCKNAGONEY

BELFAST CITY AIRPORT

BELFAST ROAD

VICTORIA PARK

SYDENHAM BY-PASS

SYDENHAM

HOLYWOOD ROAD

PARKWAY

BELMONT ROAD

BRIDGE END FLYOVER

BELMONT ROAD

BELMONT

HAWTHORNDEN WAY

A20
TO NEWTOWNARDS
9½ 6

NEWTOWNARDS ROAD

MOUNT POLLINGER RD

STRANDTOWN

ALBERTBRIDGE ROAD

UPPER NEWTOWNARDS ROAD

BALLYMACARRET

BEERSBRIDGE ROAD

BALLYHACKAMORE

WOODSTOCK ROAD

BLOOMFIELD

TULLYCARNET

GRAND PARADE

KING'S ROAD

KNOCK

GILNAHIRK ROAD

RAVENHILL ROAD

KNOCK ROAD

GILNAHIRK

ORMEAU PARK

CASTLEREAGH ROAD

LADAS DRIVE

Shandon Park
Golf Course

BRANIEL

BALLYNAFEIGH

CREGAGH ROAD

CASTLEREAGH

LOWER BRANIEL ROAD

CREGAGH

MOUNT MERRION AVENUE

UPPER KNOCKBREDA ROAD

BALLYGOWAN ROAD

Mls 0   ¼   ½
Km   ½   1

A24
TO BALLYNAHINCH 17½ 11
NEWCASTLE   41½ 26
DOWNPATRICK   29½ 18½

CORK

N20 TO MALLOW, LIMERICK

R 617 TO BLARNEY

N22 TO KILLARNEY

N600 TO BALLINCOLLIG

TOURIST OFFICE
021-273251

KNOCKNAHEENY

BLACKPOOL

Collins Barracks

Bishop's House

Hospital

Hospital

SUNDAY'S WELL

College

Opera Ho

Bus Sta

U.C.C.

Hospital

College

Cork Lough

C.I.E. Depot

Fás

Regional College

Sch

Sch

Regional Hospital

Cemetery

College

E.S.B. Offices

BISHOPSTOWN

TOGHER

BALLYPHEHANE

Golf Course

Ch

N71 TO BANDON

R600 TO AIRPORT, KINSALE

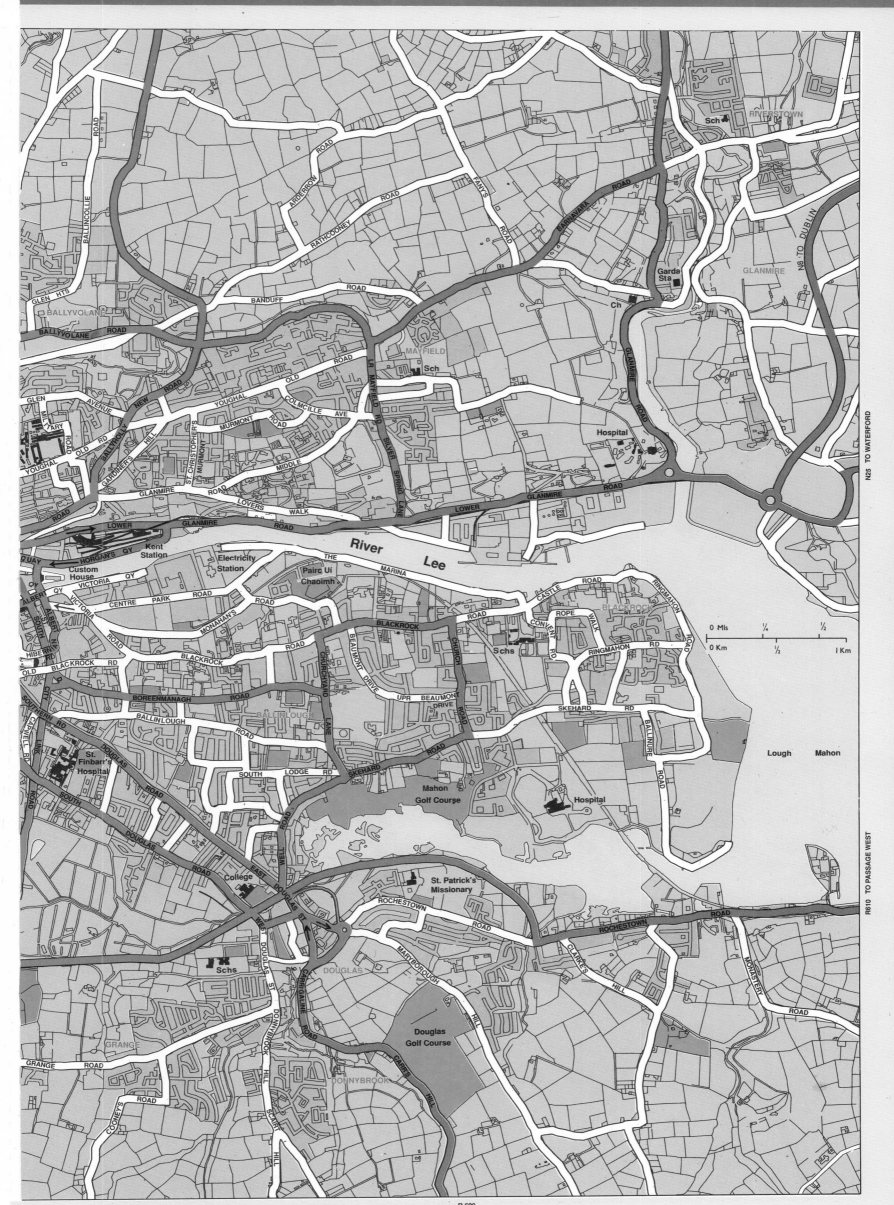

RIVERSTOWN

Sch

Sch

GLANMIRE

N8 TO DUBLIN

N25 TO WATERFORD

BALLYVOLANE

GLEN HTS

GLEN

MILITARY

YOUGHAL

OLD RD

GARDINER'S

HILL

BALLYHOOLY

NEW ROAD

ST. CHRISTOPHER'S

GLANMIRE ROAD

BALLINCOLLIG

ARDERROW

ROAD

RATHCOONEY ROAD

BANDUFF

ROAD

FANY'S ROAD

BARNAVARA ROAD

GLANMIRE ROAD

Garda Sta

Ch

MAYFIELD

Sch

LR MAYFIELD RD

YOUGHAL

COLMCILLE AVE

MURMONT

ROAD

MIDDLE

SILVER

SPRING LANE

Hospital

BALLYVOLANE ROAD

AVENUE

GLANMIRE

LOVERS WALK

THE MARINA

LOWER

GLANMIRE ROAD

LOWER

GLANMIRE ROAD

River Lee

QUAY

HORGAN'S QY

Kent Station

Electricity Station

Pairc Uí Chaoimh

Custom House

VICTORIA QY

CENTRE PARK ROAD

ROAD

ALBERT QY

HIBERNIAN

MONAHAN'S

ROAD

ROAD

CASTLE ROAD

RINGMAHON

BLACKROCK

Rope WALK

BLACKROCK RD

OLD BLACKROCK RD

BLACKROCK

ROAD

BEAUMONT DRIVE

CHURCHYARD LANE

CHURCH ROAD

CONVENT RD

Schs

RINGMAHON RD

SOUTHERN RD

CASWELL RD

CITY LINK RD

St. Finbarr's Hospital

BOREENMANAGH ROAD

BALLINLOUGH

BALLINLOUGH ROAD

UPR BEAUMONT DRIVE

SKEHARD RD

BALLINURE ROAD

Lough Mahon

DOUGLAS

ROAD

SOUTH LODGE RD

SKEHARD ROAD

Mahon Golf Course

Hospital

DOUGLAS ROAD

College

EAST DOUGLAS ST

WEST DOUGLAS ST

DONNYBROOK HILL

Schs

CARRIGALINE ROAD

St. Patrick's Missionary

ROCHESTOWN

ROCHESTOWN ROAD

ROCHESTOWN

ROAD

CLARKES HILL

MONASTERY ROAD

R610 TO PASSAGE WEST

DOUGLAS

MARYBOROUGH HILL

CARR'S HILL

GRANGE

GRANGE ROAD

COONEY'S ROAD

SCART HILL

DONNYBROOK

Douglas Golf Course

0 Mls   ¼   ½
0 Km   ½   1 Km

LONDONDERRY

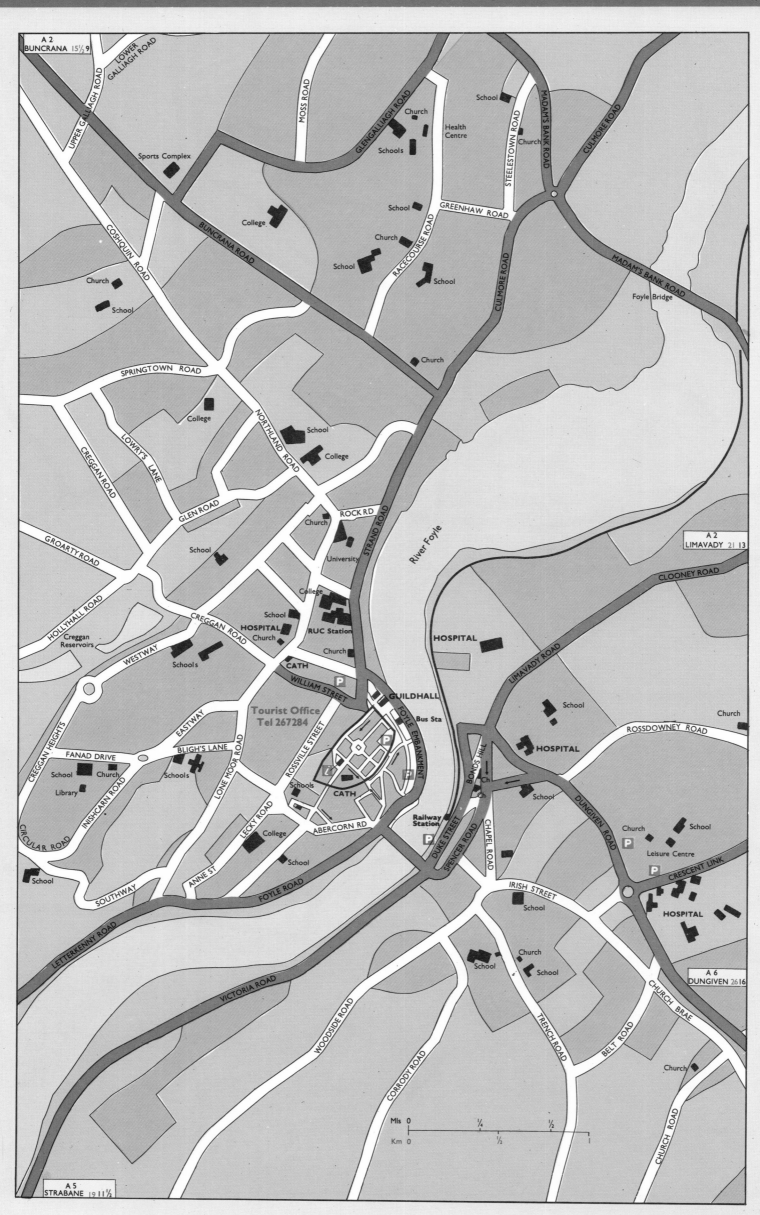

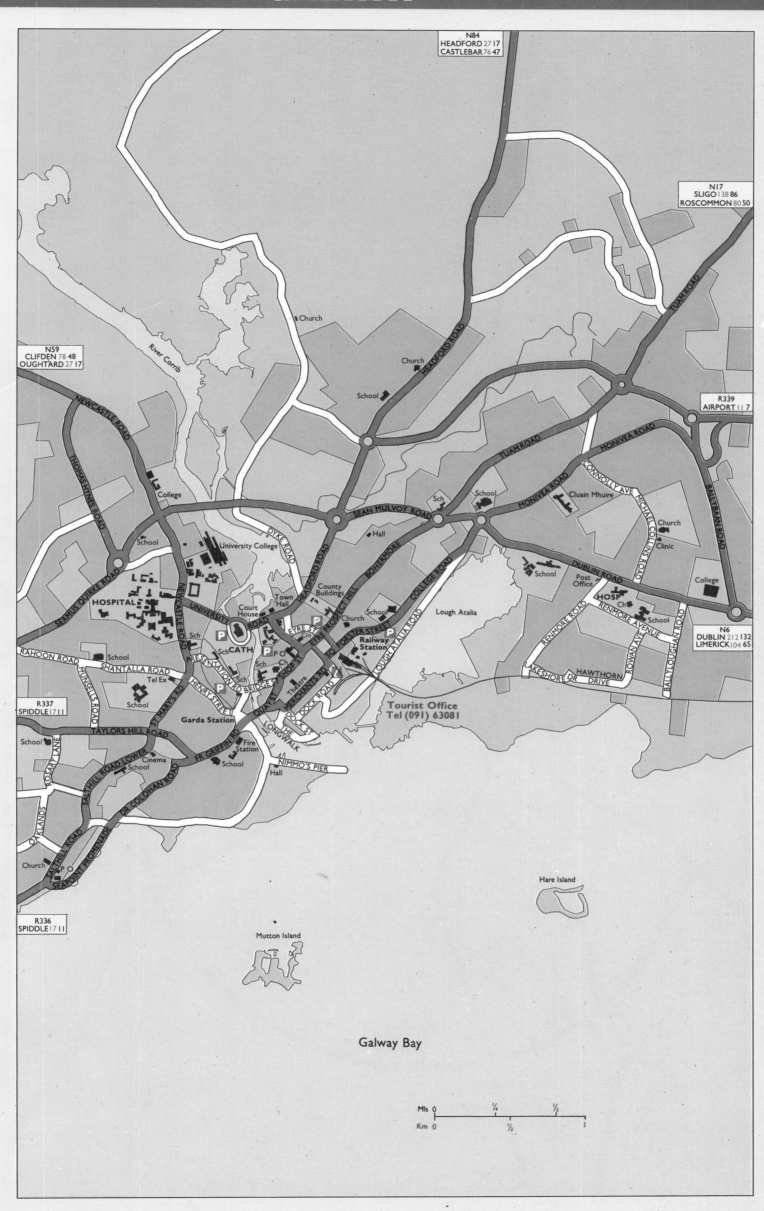

N84
HEADFORD 27 17
CASTLEBAR 76 47

N17
SLIGO 138 86
ROSCOMMON 80 50

N59
CLIFDEN 78 48
OUGHTARD 27 17

R339
AIRPORT 11 7

Church

River Corrib

Church

Church

School

NEWCASTLE ROAD

THOMAS HYNES ROAD

College

TUAM ROAD

HEADFORD ROAD

SEAN MULVOY ROAD

MONIVEA ROAD

MONIVEA ROAD

CONNOLLY AVE

MICHAEL COLLINS ROAD

BALLYBANE ROAD

School

School

Sch

School

Cluain Mhuire

Church

Clinic

College

School

DYKE ROAD

HEADFORD ROAD

BOHERMORE

DUBLIN ROAD

COLLEGE ROAD

Hall

School

Post Office

SEAMUS QUIRKE ROAD

NEWCASTLE ROAD

University College

Town Hall

County Buildings

Lough Atalia

HOSP

Ch

RENMORE ROAD

RENMORE AVENUE

School

ROWAN AV.

BALLYLOUGHAN ROAD

N6
DUBLIN 212 132
LIMERICK 104 65

HOSPITAL

UNIVERSITY ROAD

Court House

Sch

EYRE ST

EYRE STREET

SQ. FORSTER STREET

Church

School

LOUGH ATALIA ROAD

Railway Station

LAKESHORE DR

HAWTHORN DRIVE

RAHOON ROAD

MUNSELLS ROAD

SHANTALLA ROAD

School

School

PRESENTATION RD

Sch

P.O.

Sch

Ch

BRIDGE ST SHOP ST

QUAY ST

Theatre

MERCHANTS RD

DOCK ST

DOCK ROAD

Tourist Office
Tel (091) 63081

Tel Ex

St MARY'S RD

HENRY STREET

CATH

Sch

P

P

P

P

R337
SPIDDLE 17 11

School

Garda Station

TAYLORS HILL ROAD

Fire Station

THE LONGWALK

SALTHILL ROAD UPPER

Cinema

School

School

Hall

NIMMO'S PIER

ROSARY LANE

OAKLANDS

FR GRIFFIN RD

DR COLOHAN ROAD

SALTHILL ROAD

SEAPOINT PROMENADE

P.O.

Church

Hare Island

R336
SPIDDLE 17 11

Mutton Island

Galway Bay

Mls 0   ¼   ½
Km 0   ½   1

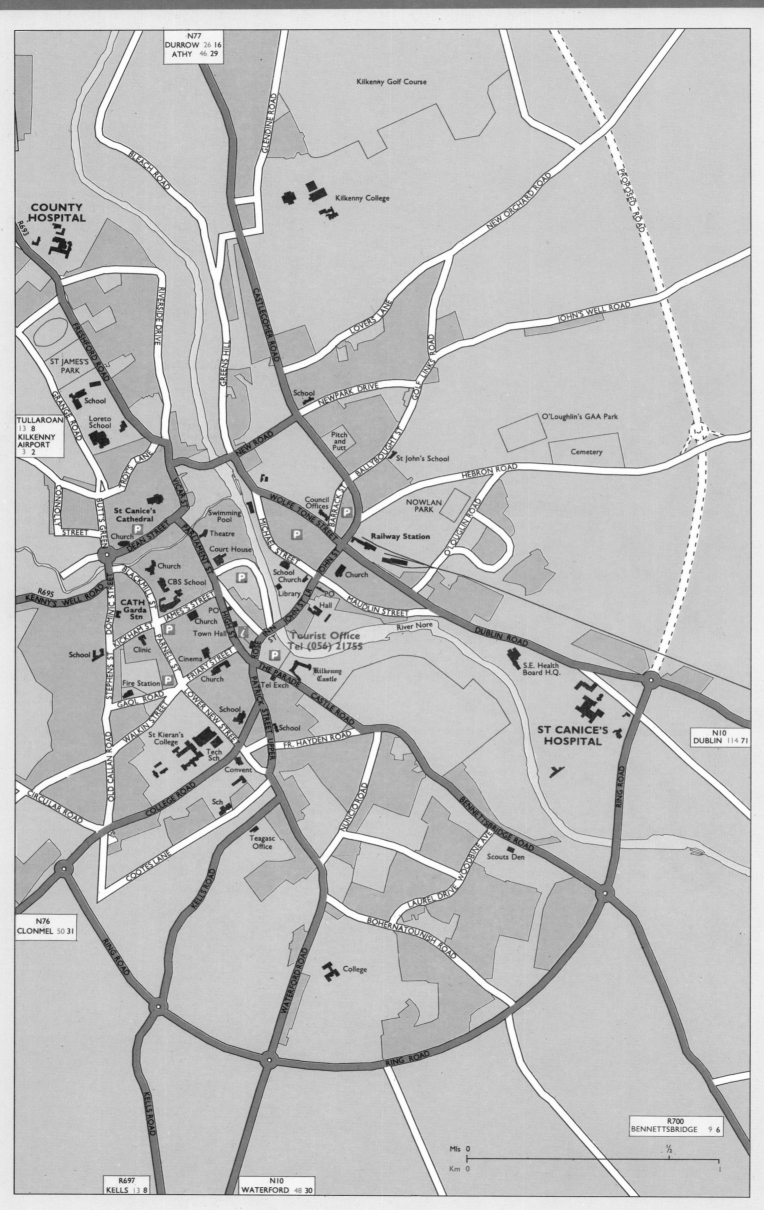

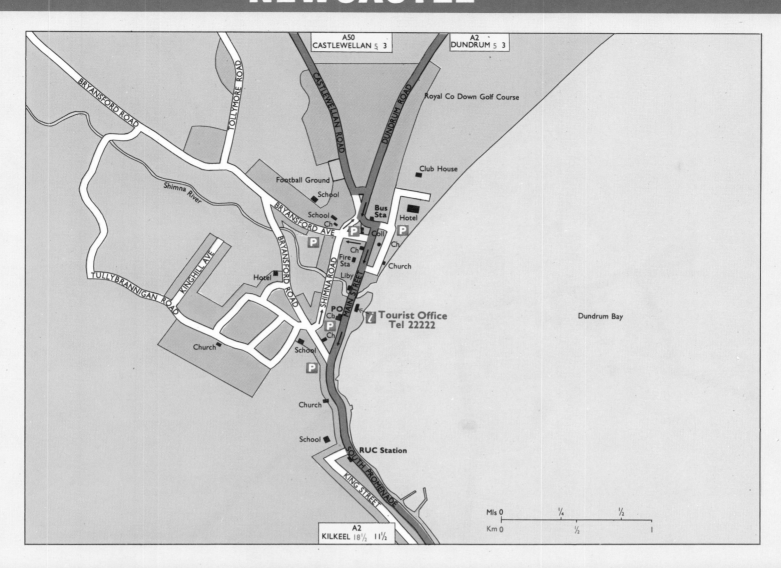

NEWRY

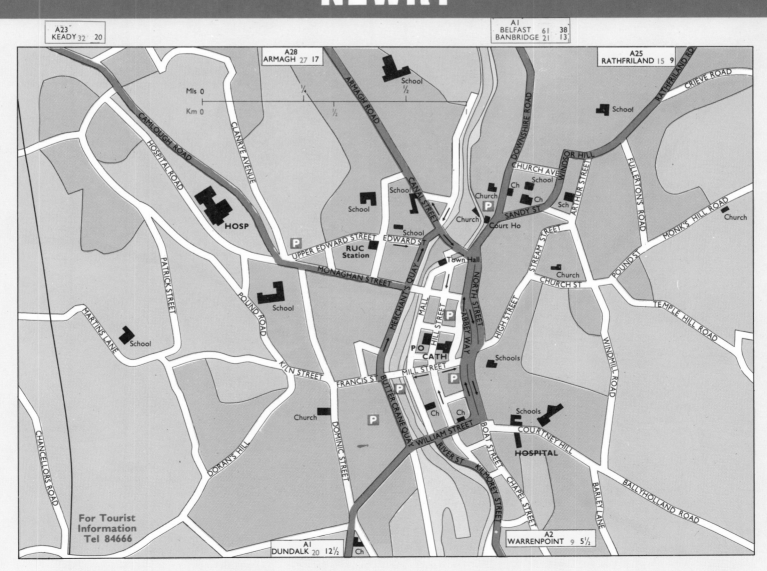

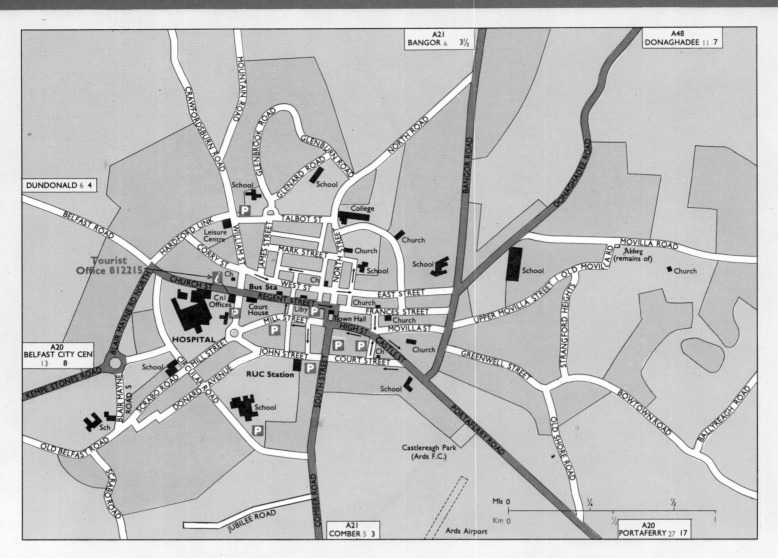

OMAGH

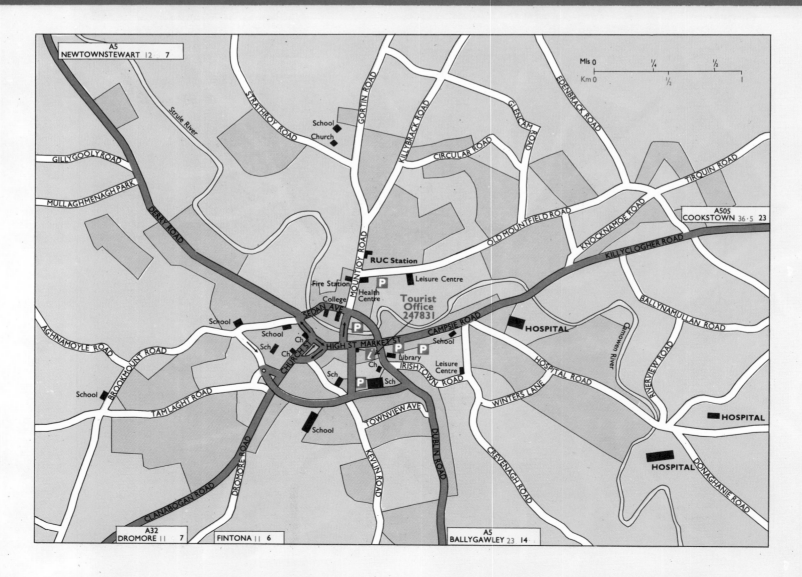

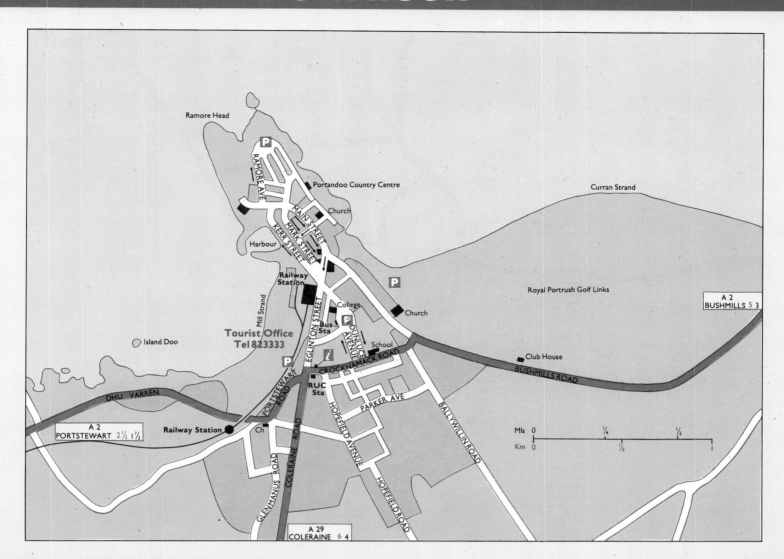

ROSSLARE HARBOUR

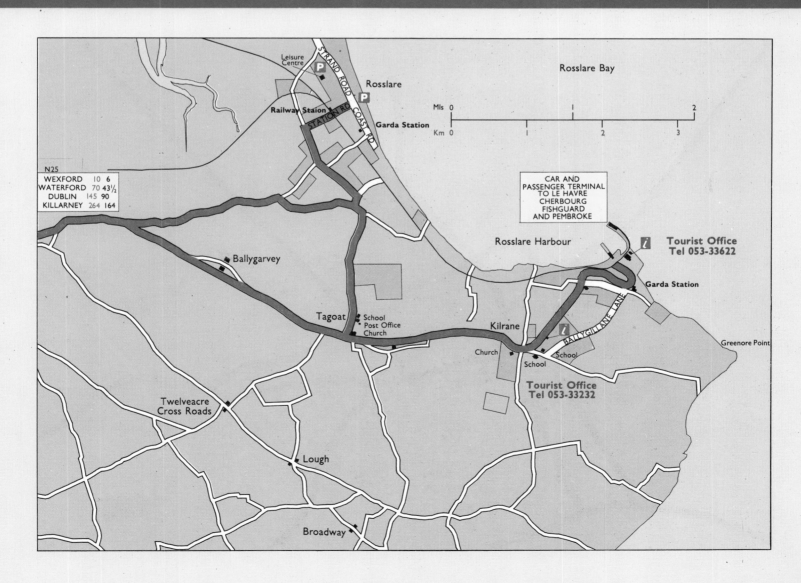

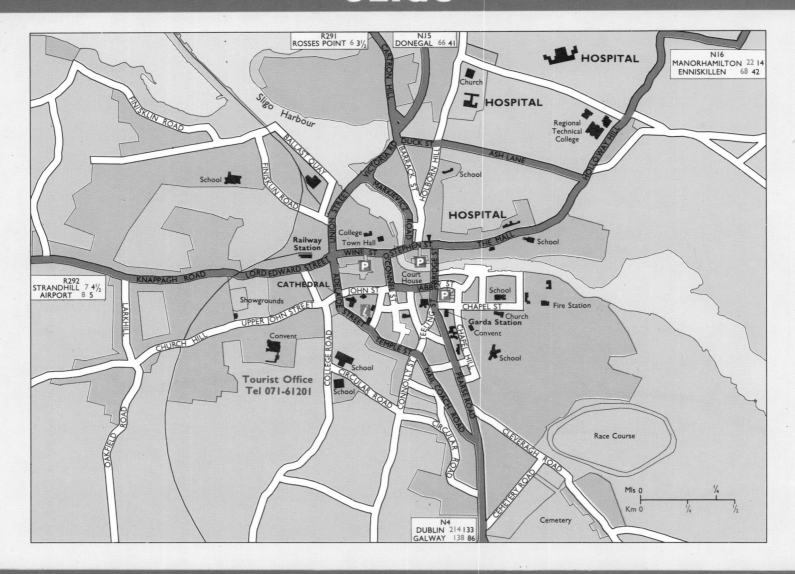

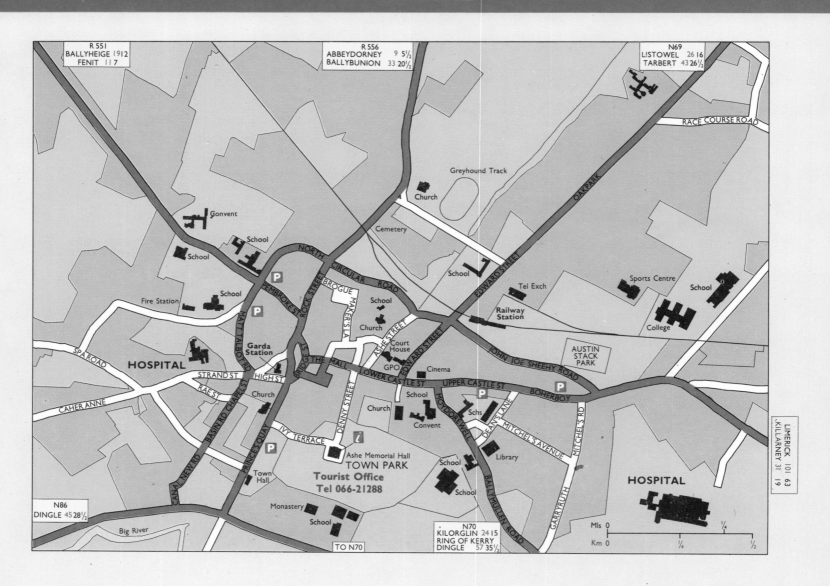

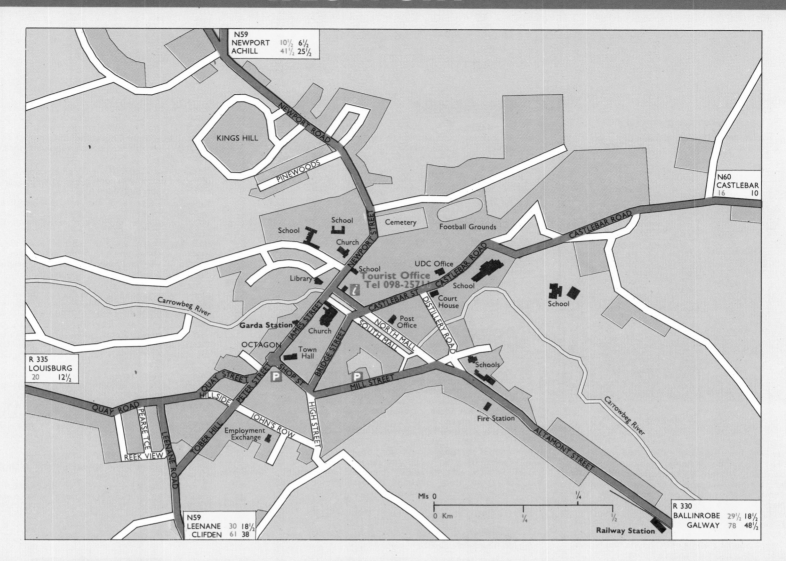

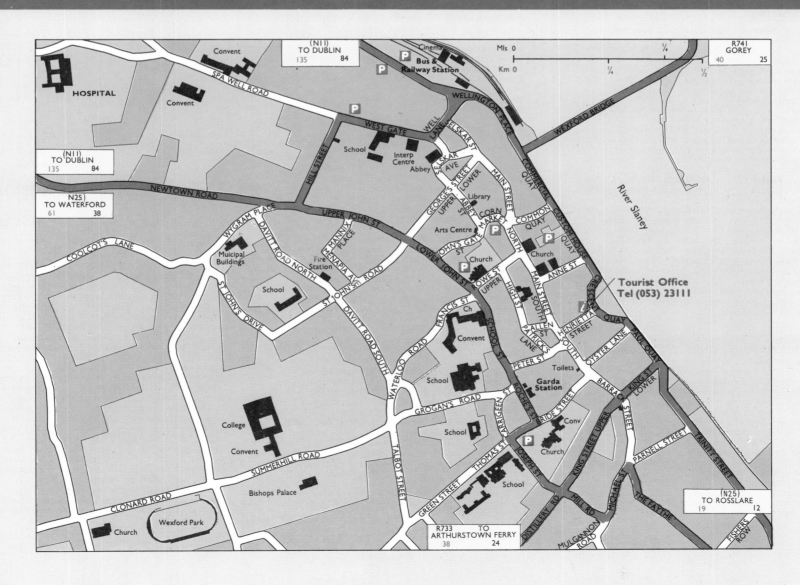

TOURING AREA 1

The river Erne, from Belturbet in Co. Cavan to Belleek on the Fermanagh-Donegal border, forms a continuous navigable waterway of about 55 miles (88 km). For most of its length it broadens to become Upper and Lower Lough Erne, several miles wide at some points and containing 154 islands. The build-up of fleets of hire cruisers has made the Fermanagh Lakeland one of Ireland's most popular holiday centres. The proximity of the lakes to the Donegal coast and the highlands and valleys of the Sperrin Mountains in Tyrone means that tourists have only short distances to travel in order to 'sample' all the traditional joys of an Irish holiday. In the west of the region the cliffs of Slieve League are the highest in Ireland and, in the east, Lough Neagh is the largest lake in the British Isles.

MUSEUMS

Donegal Museum, Franciscan Friary, Rossnowlagh (7 D3): archaeology, folklife, military history, numismatics.
Glencolumbkille Museum (7 A1): a folk village in the main Irish-speaking district of Donegal.
Enniskillen Castle (8 H5): houses the Fermanagh county museum and the regimental museum of the Royal Inniskilling Fusiliers and Dragoons, are housed in the multi period castle.
Explore Erne (8 H5): a new interpretive facility at Belleek exploring the story of Erne.
Roslea Heritage Centre (8 H5): a converted school building which houses displays of spademaking, Roslea lace and reconstructed early 20th century classroom. The centre also offers a genealogy service for County Fermanagh.
Belleek Pottery (7 E4): founded in 1857, this famous pottery produces only Irish designs and many beautiful specimens are on display in a small museum.
The Ulster-American Folk Park, Camp Hill, Omagh (8 K2): illustrates the role played in American history by tens of thousands of immigrants from Ulster, who included the forebears of a dozen US Presidents.
Devenish Monastic Site, Lower Lough Erne (8 H5): a small museum on Devenish Island explains the history of one of the most remarkable groups of ecclesiastical buildings in Ireland.
Ulster History Park, (8 K1) Cullion, Omagh: the human history of the primitive settlers in 7000BC to the end of the 17th century.

NATIONAL TRUST PROPERTIES

Florence Court (8 G6), 7 miles (11 km) south-west of Enniskillen: 18th century house of Earls of Enniskillen, with outstanding plasterwork.
Castle Coole (8 H5), Enniskillen: 18th century classical house of Earls of Belmore; architect, James Wyatt; plasterwork by Joseph Rose.
Wellbrook Beetling Mill (9 C2), 4 miles (5 km) west of Cookstown: 18th century water-powered linen beetling mill in working order.
Gray's Printing Press, Strabane (2 J7); workshop where John Dunlap, printer of the American Declaration of Independence, learned his trade.
Crom Estate (8 J7), 3 miles 3 miles west of Newtownbutler: over a thousand acres of woodland, farmland and loughs. Buildings include Crom Castle and Crighton Tower. Day ticket by arrangement with warden.

CATHEDRALS

Enniskillen, St Macartin's (8 H5): completed 1842 and incorporates 17th century tower and porch.
Clogher, St Macartan's (9 A4): neat classical edifice of 1744, where the bishop's palace, in similar style, is now a Catholic home for the old.

FOREST PARKS

Gortin Glen Forest Park (8 K1): with forest drive, lakes and deer reserve.
Drum Manor Forest Park (9 C2): has a butterfly garden.
Parkanaur Forest Park (9 C2): with woodland trails, deer park and exhibition centre.
Benburb Valley Park (9 D4): Ash, Beech and Conifers surround a limestone gorge. Ruins of Benburb Castle built on the cliff edge in 1615 tower over the river.

COUNTRY PARKS AND NATURE RESERVES

Marble Arch Cave and Glen (8 G6): the Cladagh river gushes from the mouth of one of the many interlinked subterranean caverns in the limestone plateau of Fermanagh. Several Nature Reserves in area.
Castle Archdale (8 G4): woodlands and marina, caravan park and horse riding.
Castle Caldwell (8 F3) end of Lower Lough Erne: a series of small sheltered bays with species rich fen and associated shoreline scrub. Bird observation hide.
Correl Glen (8 F4) opposite entrance to Lough Navar Scenic Drive: mixed woodland and acid heath on series of escarpments of carboniferous limestone and sandstone.

ANTIQUITIES

Abbey of Assaroe (7 D3), 1 mile (1·5 km) west of Ballyshannon: fragments of once-famous Cistercian abbey founded in 1184; many ancient headstones.
Kilbarron Castle (7 D3), 2 miles (3 km) south of Rossnowlagh: 13th-14th century ruins with, to the north, remains of 14th century Kilbarron Church on the site of the original church of St Barron, c.545.
Ard Fothadh (7 E2), 2 miles (3 km) north-west of Ballintra: also known as McGonigle's Fort; earthen rampart with beehive mound, believed to be burial place of a 6th century king, Hugh McAinmire. Other ancient tombs in the vicinity include one near Connor's Bridge, and another on the west slope of Lurgan Carn.
Donegal Castle (7 E2), in Donegal town, on bank of river Eske: in 1505 an earlier castle was rebuilt as the main stronghold of Red Hugh O'Donnell.
Donegal Abbey (7 E2), ruins of 15th century Franciscan friary.
Castle Magrath (8 F3), 1½ miles (2·5 km) from Pettigo: 16th century castle of the traditional guardians of Lough Derg monastery.
Lough Derg (8 F2): contains Station Island, traditional scene of 'St Patrick's Purgatory'; the small island has the 'penitential beds' and the remains of monks' cells, also two modern churches and hospices.
Tamlaght (8 G2), 3 miles (5 km) north of Pettigo: large oval cairn covering rectangular chamber; south-west of cairn is a dolmen and ancient burial place with a Mass shelter from penal times.
Glencolumbkille (7 A1): many pre-Christian monuments - portal grave, souterrians and cairns - dating from Bronze Age and earlier.
Malinmore (7 A1): a large number of prehistoric tombs including a fine horned cairn called Cloghanmore.
Dunmore Head (1 B7), west of Portnoo: has two ancient ring forts; a massive circular fort of stone, in good preservation, is on an island in Lough Doon 1½ miles (2·5 km) south of Portnoo.
Drumskinny Stone Circle and Cairn (8 H2), 5 miles (8 km) north of Kesh: Bronze Age ceremonial site.
Inishmacsaint Church and Cross (8 G4), on Inishmacsaint Island, Lower Lough Erne: tall undecorated cross and ruined church of several periods mark the site of an important 6th century monastery.
White Island Statues (8 G3), Lower Lough Erne, off Castle Archdale Country Park: a small ruined church of c.1200 within a large earthen enclosure contains a unique group of pre-Norman stone figures, exact date and function still disputed.
Tully Castle (8 G4): ruin of Plantation castle built by Sir John Hume. Delightful formal garden.
Monea Castle (8 G5): best surviving Fermanagh Plantation castle, 1618-19, showing strong Scottish influence, in surrounding dawn.
Castle Balfour, Lisnaskea (8 J6): ruin of Plantation castle begun about 1618 by Sir James Balfour, a Scottish planter.

Knockmany Chambered Cairn (9 A4): late neolithic burial chamber with fine display of megalithic art, on a 700 ft (212 m) hill in Knockmany Forest.
Errigal Keerogue Cross and Church (9 A4): ridge-top graveyard with ruined church and unfinished ringed cross.
Beaghmore Stone Circles (9 B1): extensive complex of circles, alignments and cairns in wild upland bog; ceremonial site of Bronze Age date.
Killymoon Castle (9 D2): one mile south east of Cookstown built in 1671 by James Stewart. Rebuilt in 1802 by architect John Nash for Colonel William Stewart.
Ballynagurragh Church, near Augher (9 A4): a window commemorates John Joseph Hughes, of the district, first archbishop of New York and builder of St Patrick's Cathedral, on Fifth Avenue.
Cregganconroe (9 B2): burial chambers with two semi-circular forecourts, good example of Ulster court grave of neolithic period; fine views of tomb.
Aghanaglack (8 F5) Dual Court Tomb 2 miles west of Boho: well preserved megalithic tomb with 2 galleries opening on to courts at either end of a rectangular cairn.
Castle Caulfield (or Caulfeild) (11 A3): ruins of imposing English-style house built by Sir Toby Caulfeild between 1611-19.
Donaghmore Cross (9 C3): made up of parts of two different crosses; decoration combines biblical and geometric motifs.
Grant House, Dergenagh (9 B3): home of the maternal ancestors of the 18th US President, Ulysses S. Grant.
Tullahogue Fort (9 D2): fine complex hilltop enclosure, headquarters and inauguration place of the O'Neills, Kings of Ulster.
Ardboe Cross (17 E5): finest northern high cross, on site of early monastery, with extensive scheme of biblical figure carving, still impressive.
Drumlane (16 J1), 4 miles (6·5 km) south of Belturbet: ruins of a 14th century church and a round tower 45 ft (13·5 m) high.

TOURING AREA 2

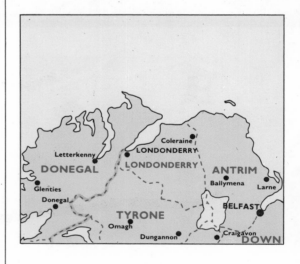

The north and north-east coastline, from Aran Island in Donegal to the Glens of Antrim deserves to be regarded by the tourist as a continuous panorama. The bare and rugged grandeur of northern Donegal gives way gradually to the white cliffs and sandy bays of North Antrim, the coast then winding southward and forming the sheltered Nine Glens whose woodlands and beach villages are still the repository of much folklore. The entire coastline's most famous place is the Giant's Causeway, a bizarre volcanic structure of basalt columns that old guidebooks habitually called 'the eighth wonder of the world'. At Bloody Foreland, the next parish to the west is in America; at Torr Head you are only 12 miles (19 km) from Scotland. The population is of mixed Irish and Scottish descent, the Macdonnells of the Scottish Isles succeeding in holding onto their Irish land after the flight of the O'Neill and O'Donnell earls in 1607. Rathlin Island, off the north-eastern tip, was for centuries considered Scottish territory; Scots Gaelic was the language of many in the Glens until the 19th century, and 'Scotch' accents dominate the region still.
This long coastal zone contains the majority of the North's golf courses, several of them world renowned. It also abounds in castles of pre- and post-Plantation date.

MUSEUMS

The Ulster Museum, Botanic Gardens, Belfast: apart from its general collections, the Ulster Museum is interesting for its galleries illustrating the landscape, natural history and archaeology of Ireland over a period of 9,000 years. It also contains the treasure recovered in 1969 at the Giant's Causeway from the surviving wreckage of the Spanish Armada galleass Girona and of Latrinidad Valencera.

Tower Museum (2 K5) in Londonderry: history of the city from prehistoric times to the present. Artefacts from Spanish Armada ships wrecked of the Irish coast in 1588 are on dislay in the O'Doherby Tower above the Museum.

Benone Tourist Complex (3 C3): along with leisure and sporting facilites the centre includes a natural history exhibition and sea-shell display

CATHEDRALS

St Columb's, Londonderry: 17th century 'Planters' Gothic' in style, with many memorials of the Plantation settlers.

St Eugene's, Londonderry: 19th century, flamboyant, good stained glass.

St Anne's, Belfast: 19th century, Hiberno-Romanesque.

St Peter's Pro-Cathedral, 19th century, dark but impressive.

FOREST PARKS

Ards Forest Park (2 F3): on Sheephaven Bay, facilities include swimming.

Glenveagh National Park (2 F5): on Garton Lough, famous deer herd.

Glenariff Forest Park (4 H4): traversed by the Ulster Way long-distance footpath, it has a nature exhibition centre and restaurant; walks by the side of waterfalls in the glen.

NATIONAL TRUST PROPERTIES

Crocknagarrack Moorland, (1 D5), near Gweedore, Co. Donegal: 6,500 acres of wild bogland with Lough na Cung.

Mussenden Temple and Bishop's Gate (3 C3): a Greek-style rotunda and classical entrance to his demesne were built by the wealthy 18th century Earl of Bristol and Bishop of Derry; walks pass the ruin of his cliff-top palace.

Springhill House, near Moneymore (9 D1): a fortified late 17th century manor house with costume museum.

The Giant's Causeway and North Antrim Cliff Path (3 E2): nearly 40,000 basalt columns and series of sheer cliffs forming bays; path of 10 miles (16 km) from the Causeway via Dunseverick Castle to White Park Bay and Ballintoy. Tea rooms and craft centre.

Carrick-a-Rede Rope Bridge (4 F2): swinging bridge to island fishery (in position May-September).

Fair Head and Murlough Bay (4 G2): cliffs and scree; sheltered and beautiful wooded bay.

Crown Liquor Saloon, Great Victoria Street, Belfast (10 J2): outstanding Victorian pub.

Rough Fort (3 B4) on the Limavady/Londonderry road: a tree ringed earth built fort. Typical defensive formsted of Celtic period.

COUNTRY PARKS AND NATURE RESERVES

Ness Country Park (3 A5): has the North's highest waterfall.

Muff Glen (3 A5): winding woodland stream and valley.

Roe Valley Country Park (3 B4): extensive area of river gorge, with reconstructed watermills and good information centre for a region of archaeological, geological and botanical interest.

Rathlin Island (4 G1): the rock stacks of the west point have major sea bird breeding colonies.

Magilligan Point (3 B3): sand dunes, myriads of sea shells, breeding area for little tern, immense beach.

Carnfunnock Country Park (4 J6) award winning park: features include maze in shape of six Counties, walled garden with auditorium time garden with unique collection of sundials, forest walks, visitors centre and camping and caravan park.

Shanes Castle Nature Reserve (11 E1) in County Antrim: has bird watching hides, deer park rare breeds, and a Camellia House.

Ulster Wildlife Trust (Benone) (3 C3)

ANTIQUITIES

Doe Castle (2 F3), on shore of Sheephaven Bay: a fortress of the MacSuibhnes in the 16th century, with rock-cut moat; adjoining graveyard has graves of Donegal chieftains.

Meevagh (2 G3), near Carrigart: ancient ruined church with Ogham stone and Latin cross.

Gortnavern (2 H3): 4 miles (6·5 km) north of Milford dolmen with huge capstone.

Buncrana (2 J3): at points around the town are a Bronze Age burial cairn, a stone circle (Crocahaisil) and a dolmen (Gransha).

St Mura's Cross (2 J4): fine example of interlaced stone carving, in graveyard of 7th century abbey (few traces) at Fahan.

The Grianan of Aileach (2 J5), 7 miles (11 km) south of Fahan: Ulster's most interesting relic - a huge, circular stone fort, built about 1700 BC as residence of the O'Neills, Kings of Ulster; 77 ft (23 m) across, terraced on the inside, with passages in the thick walls. Magnificent views of Lough Swilly.

Donagh Cross (2 K2), west of Carndonagh: also called St Patrick's Cross, probably the oldest low-relief cross still standing in Ireland.

Cooley Graveyard (3 A2), 2 miles (3 km) north west of Moville: reputed burial place of St Finian; has remains of an ancient church, a structure called 'the skull house', an unusual stone cross and a monolithic cross 10 ft (3 m) high.

Martellow Tower (3 B3), this tower is situated at Magilligan Point.

Kings Fort (3 C4): one of the best preserved Raths in Ulster.

Londonderry City Walls (2 K5): completed in 1618, nearly 1 mile (1·5 km) in circuit, still intact, with cannon and bastions.

Banagher Church (3 B6): nave of c.1100, chancel soon after 1200, an impressive ruin, traditional source of 'lucky sand'.

Dungiven Priory (3 B6): complex ruin on site of early monastery and medieval priory of Augustinian canon, with fine 15th century tomb of Cooey-na-Gall O'Cahan, and medieval tower house reused in 17th century in fortified house and bawn.

Mountsandel (3 D3): splendid mound dominating the wooded Bann Valley; date and function uncertain, but traces of mesolithic huts at base.

Ballylumford Dolmen, Islandmagee (4 K6): popularly called the druids' altar, this neolithic monument is in the garden of a house.

Carrickfergus Castle (12 H1): one of the finest castles in Ireland, begun c.1180 by John de Courcy, Anglo-Norman invader of Ulster; of military importance for seven centuries.

President Jackson Centre, Carrickfergus (12 H1): near site of the home of the grandparents of 7th US President, Andrew Jackson ('Old Hickory').

McArt's Fort (12 G2): spectacularly situated fort on the summit of Cave Hill (1,100 ft, 335m) where the United Irishmen's leaders took an oath in 1798.

Tirorny (3 D6): Portal tomb, Neolithic site at roadside 1¾ miles north west of Maghera.

Tirkane (3 D6): sweat house 2¼ miles north west of Maghera

Maghera Old Church (3 D7): much altered church with fine carved west door, and St Lurach's grave nearby.

Dunluce Castle (3 E2): spectacularly sited ruins of 15th-16th century main castle of the Scottish MacDonnells of Antrim.

Dunseverick Castle (3 E2): only one wall, on rocky peninsula, remains of one of Ireland's oldest strongholds, linked with Emain Macha and Tara.

Kinbane Castle (4 F2): picturesquely sited 16th century castle of the MacDonnells.

Bonamargy Friary (4 G2): extensive ruins of Franciscan friary, founded c.1500, with burial vault of the MacDonnells.

Ballypatrick Cairn (4 G3), on the scenic drive in Ballypatrick Forest: fine neolithic dual court with long cairn and forecourt at each end.

Doey's Cairn, Dunloy (4 F5): neolithic court tomb.

Ossian's Grave (4 H4): beautifully situated neolithic burial site, locally linked with legendary Celtic poet Ossian.

Arthur House, Cullybackey (4 F6): was the home of the parents of 21st US President, Chester Alan Arthur.

Ballygally Castle (4 J6): Scottish-style castle built c.1625 by James Shaw of Greenock; one of Ulster's few 17th century buildings still in use.

Antrim Round Tower (11 E1): well-preserved tower, 93 ft (18 m) high, only surviving feature of an important early monastery.

Cranfield Church (11 D1): 13th century ruin on shore of Lough Neagh, with holy well visited for 'lucky pebbles'.

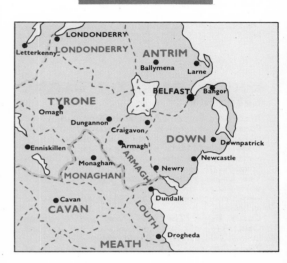

TOURING AREA 3

Within a radius of 60 miles (96 km) around Carlingford Lough, there lies a great variety of scenery and interest. Co. Monaghan is noted for coarse fishing in numerous lakes that form a chain into South Armagh. Carlingford Lough divides the Cooley Mountains from the Mountains of Mourne, main scene of the Ulster Cycle of epic poems. Armagh city, with its two cathedrals, has been the ecclesiastical capital of Ireland since St Patrick chose it. To the west, Strangford Lough (an enormous bird sanctuary) provided the saint's landing place on his mission to Ireland in AD 432. Downpatrick, near the Lough shore, claims his last resting place.

MUSEUMS

Lisburn Museum (12 F3): award-winning museum where the story of the Linen Industry is on permanent display.

Monaghan County Museum (9 B6): the Courthouse, Monaghan: archaeology, folklife, local history.

Armagh County Museum (9 D5): The Mall, Armagh: local history and archaeology, paintings, by Æ. (George Russell).

Royal Irish Fusiliers Museum (9 D5); the Mall, Armagh; military history.

Cathedral Library (9 D5): adjoining the Protestant Cathedral, Armagh: books, manuscripts, ecclesiastical items.

The Planetarium and Hall of Astronomy (9 D5): College Hill, Armagh: astronomy and space travel. Saturday shows.

The Ulster Folk and Transport Museum (10 K1), Cultra, Co Down: reconstructions of rural dwellings, collection of locomotives, old vehicles, the linen and shipbuilding industries, country crafts, souvenir shop. All in a large park.

North Down Heritage Centre (12 J1): Local Museum and Art Gallery situated at rear of town hall, Bangor.

Down County Museum (12 H5) in Downpatrick: Stone age artefacts and Bronze age gold found locally are displayed in this former jail. The story of St Patrick is featured in one of the gatehouses.

NATIONAL TRUST PROPERTIES

Ardress House (9 E4), 7 miles (11 km) west of Portadown: 17th-18th century house with fine plasterwork by Michael Stapleton.

Rowallane (12 H4), Saintfield: 217 acres of gardens, noted for rare trees and flowers.

Castle Ward (12 J5), Strangford: 18th century mansion of Lord and Lady Bangor with contrasting facades and fascinating furnishings; gardens, lake, wildfowl, goldsmith's workshop, Victorian laundry, tower house, classical 'folly', etc.

Mount Stewart House and Gardens (12 J2), near Greyabbey: was the home of the famous Lord Castlereagh; the Adam-style house has interesting relics; the gardens have extraordinary 'Noah's Ark' Statues and lake vistas. The grounds contain the Temple of the Winds, a Grecian 'folly', and Tir na nOg, a family burial ground.

Kearney and Knockinelder (12 K4): a preserved coastal village.
Anne's Point, Greyabbey (12 J3): 14 acres of arable land with one acre of shoreline adjoining to other NT properties.
Ballykeel (The Gobbins) (4 K7): 36 acres of diverse coarse, semi improved grassland.
Slieve Donard (10 J7): Horseshoe of upland extends to 1300 acres and includes summits and northern slopes of Slieve Donard and Slieve Commedagh.
Greyabbey Bay (12 J3): 3608 acres of land foreshore and sea beach situated south of properties owned by NT.

COUNTRY PARKS AND NATURE RESERVES

Bracknagh Bog and Peatlands Park (11 C3), near Portadown: an extensive marshy region near the south shore of Lough Neagh, noted for rare plants.
Oxford Island Nature Reserve (11 D3), near Lurgan: a marina with nature trails, on south-west shore of Lough Neagh.
The Lagan Valley Regional Park (12 G3): the winding Lagan river, with towpath, locks, bridges and woods, constitute a lovely 'lung' all the way from Belfast to Lisburn.
Castle Espie (The Wild Fowl and Wetlands Centre) (12 H3): Bird Sanctuary and breeding ground for wild fowl. Largest wild fowl collection in Ireland.
Moira Demesne (11 E3) : 44 acre park famous for its rose displays incorporating caravan park. Nearby is oldest surviving railway station in Ulster (1841)
Mourne Coastal Path (12 G7), south of Newcastle: extends along the rocky shore and up the side of the Bloody Bridge river towards the top of Slieve Donard or though the Mournes by the Brandy Pad.
Murlough Nature Reserve (12 H6), Dundrum: extensive sand dunes and heathland, with long beach.
Quoile Pondage (12 H5), Downpatrick: beautiful stretch of wide river with flocks of ducks, geese and swans.
Scrabo Tower and Country Park (12 H5), Newtownards: steep woodlands surmounted by Gothic tower memorial to Lord Castlereagh's brother.
Copeland Islands (12 J1): bird sanctuary visitable from Donaghadee.
Coney Island (11 C3), Lough Neagh: bird sanctuary visitable from Maghery.
Crawfordsburn Country Park (12 H1): delightful open shore and woodlands on south side Belfast Lough.
Silent Valley (10 J7), near to Kilkeel : The Silent Valley and Ben Crom Reservoirs supply 30 million gallons of water a day to Belfast and County Down. There is an area of beautiful parkland before reaching the dams.
Ulster Wildlife Centre (12 H4) : in Crossgar, County Down, learn about wildlife on the wetland, raised bog and meadowland of Tobar Mhuire Monastery.
North Down Coastal Path (12 H1 - 12 J1) : One of North Down's most important recreational resources. Runs 15 miles along the southern shore of Belfast Lough from Holywood to Portavoe.

FOREST PARKS

Rossmore Forest Park (9 B6), 1 mile (1·5 km) south of Monaghan: forest and lakeshore nature trails, fishing.
Gosford Forest Park (9 E5), Markethill: Gosford Castle, Norman Revival extravaganza of the 2nd Earl, was 'the biggest private house in Ireland'.
Tollymore Forest Park (10 J6), Newcastle: splendid trees on the slopes of the Mournes and several 'follies'.
Castlewellan Forest Park (10 J6): lake and outstanding arboretum.
Slieve Gullion Forest Park (10 F7), 4 miles (6·5 km) west of Newry: has a 7 miles (11·26 km) forest drive with some of the finest views in Ireland.

CATHEDRALS

St Patrick's Anglican Cathedral (9 D5), Armagh: on a rath where the present streets follow the Celtic ramparts; Brian Boru was buried here (1014); interesting statuary and gargoyles.
St Patrick's Catholic Cathedral (9 D5), Armagh: reached by a fine flight of steps; took 70 years to build, owing to the Great Famine. Noted for colourful mosaics and carvings of angels and saints.
Cathedral Church of the Holy Trinity (10 K5), Downpatrick: Anglican; small successor of several destroyed since St Patrick first built a church here; tradition claims not only the grave of St Patrick but that the bones of St Brigid and St Columba were brought by de Courcy to rest here.

Cathedral Church of Christ the Redeemer (10 H4), Dromore: Anglican; small, with tomb of Bishop Jeremy Taylor.
Cathedral of SS Patrick and Colman (10 F7), Newry: Catholic; light and pleasant Tudor-Gothic edifice of Newry granite (1825).

ANTIQUITIES

Clones, Co. Monaghan (9 A7): contains a well preserved round tower; Celtic cross in centre of town.
Cootehill, Co Cavan (17 B1): a prehistoric tomb of the court cairn type, 3 miles (5 km) along the Shercock road.
King John's Castle, Carlingford, Co. Louth (18 G1): massive fortress overlooking the harbour, possibly on site of a much older structure; 14th century Dominican abbey.
Taaffe's Castle, also in Carlingford (18 G1): a large square keep, in good preservation, probably 16th century. Off the main square are the Mint, a 16th century fortified house, and the Tholsel, an ancient archway originally a gate tower in the town wall of which there are some remains. The Rectory and Ghan House are noteworthy 18th century residences.
Tynan Cross (9 C5): formed of parts of two Celtic crosses, with carvings including Adam and Eve.
Navan Fort (9 D5): impressive hilltop enclosure identified as Emain Macha, Ulster rival of Tara, 'palace' of the Red Branch Knights. Visitor Centre open 1993.
Armagh Friary (9 D5): ruined church of 13th century Franciscan Friary, the longest friary church in Ireland.
Annaghmare Cairn (17 E1): fine court tomb illustrating neolithic construction technique.
Ballykeel Dolmen (9 E7): portal grave and cist at either end of long cairn, at western foot of Slieve Gullion.
Slieve Gullion Cairns (10 F7): on summit of Slieve Gullion (1,920 ft, 576 m), south cairn neolithic, north cairn Bronze Age; reached by forest drive, and strenuous climb following rough path.
Killevy Churches (10 F7): ruins of two churches (pre-Norman and medieval) on site of one of Ireland's most important early nunneries.
Moyry Castle (18 F1): 3-storey square tower built 1601 to guard 'the gap of the North'.
Kilnasaggart Inscribed Stone (18 F1): granite pillar with Irish inscription and carvings, datable to c.700.
Ross Memorial (18 G1): tall obelisk narrating the career of Maj. Gen. Robert Ross, of Rostrevor, who burned the White House, Washington, in the Anglo-American War of 1812.
Greencastle (18 H1): royal castle built in 13th century, commanding entrance to Carlingford Lough; earlier motte nearby.
Legananny Dolmen (10 H5): Ulster's most graceful portal grave, at 850 ft (258·5 m) with fine views.
Drumena Cashel (10 J6): well preserved stone farmstead enclosure of Early Christian period, with souterrain and traces of huts.
Maghera Old Church and Round Tower (10 J6): ruins on site of 6th century monastery.
Dundrum Castle (10 K6): impressive remains of castle begun by John de Courcy in late 12th century; circular keep and two baileys; splendid view of Mourne Mountains.
Loughinisland Churches (10 K5): ruins of three churches 13th-16th centuries, on a lake island reached by a causeway.
Dromore Mound (10 H4): magnificent Anglo-Norman earthwork castle in bend of river Lagan.
Hillsborough (10 H4): attractive Georgian village with artillery fort, market house, parish church and former governor's mansion.
St John's Point Church (12 J6): ruin of small 10th-11th century church.
Jordan's Castle (12 J6): best preserved of five 15th-16th century merchants' tower houses in the small port of Ardglass.
Ballynoe Stone Circle (12 H5): late neolithic burial and ritual structure.
Strueil Wells (12 J5): healing wells and bath houses associated with St Patrick, well preserved.
St Patrick's Grave (12 H5): a monolith of Mourne granite, in churchyard of Downpatrick cathedral, the saint's supposed burial place.
Inch Abbey (12 H5): ruins of 12th century Cistercian abbey on river bank.
Audley's Castle (12 J4): well preserved tower-house overlooking Strangford Lough.
Quoile Castle (12 H5) : tower house.
Mound of Down (12 H5): massive earthwork, possibley a local capital, taken over by Anglo-Normans during conquest of Ulster.
Audleystown Cairn (12 J4): neolithic dual court grave.
Narrow Water Castle (18 G1): tower-house in bawn, built c.1560, beautifully situated at entrance to Newry estuary.
Kilclief Castle (12 J5): 15th century tower house on seashore, possible model for many similar throughout Ulster. Several others nearby.
Strangford Castle (12 J5): 16th century tower house.
Sketrick Castle (12 J3): ruin of tall 15th century tower house.

Nendrum Monastic Site (12 J3): pre-Norman monastery with remains of enclosures, church, round tower and cells, on a near-island with visitor centre.
Ballycopeland Windmill (12 J2): fine 18th century windmill with wooden machinery in working order.
Grey Abbey (12 J3): ruins of Cistercian abbey founded in 1193 by Affreca, wife of John de Courcy, with her carved tomb.
Kirkistown Castle (12 K4): 17th century tower-house and bawn.
The Kempe Stones (12 H2): fine portal tomb in Belfast suburb.
The Giant's Ring (12 G3): circular embanked enclosure, over 600 ft (182·5 m) in diameter, with dolmen in the middle. Probably neolithic and Bronze age passage tomb assembly site.
Tower House (12 J1) Bangor: built 1637 as a custom house with flanking towers.
Bangor Abbey (12 J1): rebuilt 1617. The tower dates back to the 14th century. The original abbey was founded by Comgall in 558AD.
Holywood Priory (12 G2): the remains of the priory date from the early 13th century.
Bangor Castle (12 J1): an impressive building functioning now as North Down's Town Hall. Built 1852.
Movilla Abbey (12 J2): one of Ulster's most important monasteries.
The Priory (12 J2): these substantial remains of a Dominician (Black) Friary founded in 1244 are the only ones of their type in Northern Ireland.
St Cooey's Wells: (8 J5) founded in 7th century by St Cooey: foundations of a church, small cemetery, modern alter and three holy wells.

TOURING AREA 4

Donegal Bay is the North's largest sea inlet and most of its southern coast is in Co. Sligo, with Leitrim and western Cavan extending eastward. Sligo town, ancient and full of interest, is also conveniently close to many beautiful sandy beaches. The many lakes in the area include Lough Gill, in which is the lake isle of Innisfree, immortalised in Yeats' poem. Leitrim and Cavan are mountainous, the range straddling the political border with Co. Fermanagh. The highest peak Cuilcagh (2,223 ft, 667 m) is right on the border. Anglers have abundance of sport, and lovers of Yeats' poetry find many associations with his youth in the area and also his grave at Drumcliff.

MUSEUM

Sligo County Museum (7 B6), Stephen Street, Sligo: folklife, archaeology, history, paintings, rare painted books, manuscripts; section on W.B. Yeats.

HISTORIC IRISH HOUSE

Lissadell House (7 B5), 8 miles (13 km) north of Sligo on Bundoran road (N 15): former home of Eva Gore-Booth and Constance Markievicz and still home of the Gore-Booth family. Many associations with W.B. Yeats. (Open daily 1 May—30 September, except Sundays, 2.30 p.m. to 5.15 p.m.)

ANTIQUITIES

Sligo Abbey (7 C6), Sligo town: Dominican abbey founded 1252 and destroyed by fire 1414; the present ruin dates from the rebellion of 1641 and the sack of Sligo; beautiful examples of Irish medieval stone carving. The most ancient of Sligo's churches is the 17th century St John's Church.

Formoyle, 4 miles (6·5 km) east of Sligo (7 C6): immense megalithic tomb of Leacht Con Mhic Ruis.

Carrowmore (7 C6), 2 miles (3 km) west of Sligo: a low hill with the largest group of megalithic remains in Ireland - dolmens, stone circles and cairns with sepulchral chambers.

Drumcliff (7 B5), 4 miles (6·5 km) north of Sligo: ancient cross by roadside with particularly good panel of Adam and Eve; close by is lower portion of a round tower. In the nearby churchyard is the grave of W.B. Yeats.

Queen Maeve's Mound (7 B6), on Knocknarea Hill, 4 miles (6·5 km) west of Sligo; a gigantic cairn said to commemorate a queen of Connaught in the first century AD.

Parkes Castle (7 C6), 5 miles (8 km) east of Sligo: ruined Plantation castle and bawn, on the east shore of Lough Gill with view of 'the lake isle of Innisfree'.

Hollybrook (15 C1), on the west shore of Lough Arrow: here is the ancient church of Aghanagh. (This district was the setting for the romantic stories of 'the Colleen Bawn'.)

Carrowkeel (15 C1), on a hilltop west of Lough Arrow: remains of a Stone Age village.

Heapstown Cairn (15 C1), 2 miles (3 km) north-east of Castlebaldwin: probably a Bronze Age monument marking the grave of a high king.

Ballymote (15 B1): has the ruins of a massive castle built in 1300 by Richard de Burgh, Red Earl of Ulster, and also of a Franciscan friary where the Book of Ballymóte was compiled in 1391.

Dromahair (7 C6): Old Hall, built in 1626, adjoins the ruins of Breffni Castle, on the river Bonet; on the opposite bank are the ruins of Creevelea Abbey (Franciscan) founded in 1508.

Manorhamilton (7 D6): has the ruins of a baronial mansion built in 1638 by Sir Frederick Hamilton.

Corracloona (7 E5), 10 miles (17 km) east of Manorhamilton: a gallery grave is surrounded by visible earthworks of the Black Pig's Dyke, supposed prehistoric frontier of Ulster.

Lough Allen (7 E7): on the island of Inismagrath, near the northern end of the lake, is a ruined church said to have been founded by St Beoy. At Tarmon, near the west shore, is a ruined church believed to have been built by one of the O'Rourkes.

Burren (P8 F6): 4 miles (6·5 km) south of Belcoo (village astride the Fermanagh-Donegal border) has a group of five chamber tombs at an altitude of 800 ft (243 m).

TOURING AREA 5

Mayo is one of Ireland's largest counties. Within its boundaries it incorporates an amazing variety of scenery, ranging from the plains of the east to the highlands of the west. Towering over the western part of the county is the cone-shaped mass of Croagh Patrick, a famous pilgrimage mountain which rises above the island-studded Clew Bay. Mayo's long coastline stretches from Killala Bay in the north to the fjord of Killary Harbour in the south where it joins up with the Connemara region of Co. Galway. It is an area of infinite variety, being a combination of islands, cliffs, rivers, lakes and long beaches. Above all, this county is known for its unspoilt traditional character. To explore off the beaten track or to visit the towns of Castlebar, Westport, Ballina or Ballinrobe is always a pleasure, as this is the centre of Ireland's 'western world'. For the angler, climber, golfer or motorist, Co. Mayo is a must. All points within the area may be reached from Westport.

ANTIQUITIES

Turlough Round Tower (14 H3): a well-preserved tower with a 17th century church standing beside it.

Strade Franciscan Friary (14 H3): remains of a 13th century friary, featuring a beautiful 15th century tomb and a fine figured altar.

Round Tower at Balla (14 H4): this broken tower is located in an old graveyard in the village.

Ballintober Abbey (14 G5): the only royal abbey in Ireland in continuous use of over 750 years; founded in 1216 by Cathal O'Connor for the Canons Regular of St Augustine. Despite suppression by Henry VIII, divine worship continued within the Abbey walls. The building was damaged by the Cromwellians in 1653. A magnificent restoration of the church was completed in 1966, the year of the Abbey's 750th anniversary.

Burriscarra Abbey (14 G5): founded in 1298 by the McEvillys for the Carmelite Order. Many interesting features.

Inishmaine Island (14 G6): this island on Lough Mask has an interesting transitional church, occupying the site of a 7th century monastery.

Cong Abbey (14 G7): dating from the 12th century, this Abbey has an impressive door of four courses with medieval stone carving. The east window is also worth seeing.

Market Cross, Cong (14 G7): first erected in the 14th century; bears an inscription in medieval Irish.

Dry Canal (14 G7): 4 miles (6·5 km) long with cut-stone banks and locks. The canal's porous bed rendered it a complete failure soon after its ceremonial opening in the mid 19th century. Situated at Cong.

Inchagoill Island (20 G1): this monastic settlement on Lough Corrib can be reached by boat from Cong.

Aghalahard Castle (14 G7): built by the de Burgos in the 15th century, later occupied by the McDonnells.

Meelick Round Tower (14 J3): marking the site of an early monastic foundation of St Broccaidh, this capless tower is 60 ft (18 m) high.

Aughagower Tower and Church (14 F4): ruins consist of a 12th century round tower and 13th century church with 15th century features.

Burrishoole Friary (13 E3): well-preserved church built by Richard Burke c.1450.

Kilgeever Abbey (13 D4): located near Louisburgh, this ancient church and holy well has a long tradition as a pilgrimage centre.

Murrisk Abbey (13 E4): an Augustinian friary dating from 1457.

Clare Island (13 C4): there are several interesting antiquities on this island, including a 15th century church, a promontory fort, a holy well and a signal tower.

Caher Island (13 B5): Early Christian remains.

Achill Island (13 B2): there are notable chamber tombs at Slievemore to the north. Kildavnet in the south is the site of an ancient castle and church.

Ardnaree Church (14 H1): this 14th century Augustinian church crowns the hill of Ardnaree.

Rosserk Abbey (6 H7): a well-preserved Franciscan tertiary friary of the 15th century.

Killala Round Tower (6 H7): part of the monastic foundation of St Muireadach.

Carbad More (6 G6): a dual full-court cairn with two gallery-graves.

Rathfranpark (6 G6): remains of a 13th century Dominican priory.

Breastagh Ogham Stone (6 G6): this tall stone is 7 miles (11 km) from Killala.

Errew Abbey (14 G1): founded by St Tiernan and later became an Augustinian friary.

Ballycastle Archaeological Remains (6 F6): digs revealing traces of farming activity dating back 5,000 years.

Bunatrahir Bay (6 G6): site of two court cairns and two dolmens.

Downpatrick Head (6 G5): remains of St Patrick's church and holy well.

Doonfeeney Upper (6 F6): two ancient graveyards with a ruined early church in one and an inscribed pillar-stone in the other. A large ring fort stands to the north-east.

Poulnachantinny (6 G5): this is the name of a puffing hole near Downpatrick Head. Nearby is the promontory fort Doonbristy.

Behy (6 F5): neolithic court cairn. Remains of two promontory forts three miles (5 km) north-west.

Doonamo Fort (5 B6): stone fort set on cliffs.

Fallmore (13 B1): remains of foundation of St Derival. Includes a small church and a holy well called St Derival's Vat.

Inishglora Island (5 B6): has 6th century monastic remains of St Brendan the Navigator. These include a monastery, nunnery, chapel and beehive hut. Some early cross slabs and stones.

Inishkea North and South Islands (5 A7): located on the north island are the extensive monastic remains of St Colmcille (died 581). Further Early Christian items on nearby Inishkea South.

Duvillaun More Island (13 A1): a small oratory within a stone enclosure and five partly collapsed beehive huts can be seen.

Dun Domhnall (5 C7): located at Glencastle 6 miles (9·5 km) from Belmullet, this stone fort stands near the 'Gates of Erris'. 'Domhnall's Grave' is beside the fort.

The Ceide Fields (6 F5): above the Atlantic on the north cost of Mayo lies the oldest known enclosed farmland in the workd 8km west of Ballycastle.

FOREST PARKS AND WALKS

For full details see 'The Open Forest', a publication available from all tourist information offices.

HOUSES, CASTLE AND GARDENS

Westport House (13 E4): home of the Marquess of Sligo. Georgian mansion with plasterwork by James Wyatt. Overlooks Clew Bay. Collection of pictures, silver, furniture etc.

MUSEUM

Knock (14 J4): sections devoted to folklife, history, archaeology and religion.

LITERARY ASSOCIATIONS

George Moore (1853-1933) was born at Moorehall House on Lough Carra, near Castlebar. Killeadan near Kiltimagh was the birthplace of blind Raftery the distinguished Irish poet who died c.1834.

TOURING AREA 6

Galway is Ireland's second largest county, extending from the Atlantic coast to the banks of the river Shannon.

For the visitor who likes a total contrast within a comparatively short travelling distance, Co. Galway is the ideal place to visit. Geographically, the county is naturally divided by the excellent fishing lake of Lough Corrib which covers an area of 68 square miles north of Galway city. To the west of this lake is the famous region known as Connemara. This area is a paradise of mountain, lakes and coastal scenery, the central features being the peaks of the Twelve Bens which are visible throughout Connemara. It is an area which has inspired generations of landscape artists who have tried to capture on canvas the region's unique charm. For the linguist it has great appeal, being populated largely by people who use Irish as their everyday language. Ireland's true traditional lifestyle may be experienced by taking a trip by air or sea to the Aran Islands which are grouped together at the entrace to Galway Bay.

The eastern part of the county consists of a large limestone plain extending to the Shannon and southwards to Co. Clare.

All points in the county may be reached from Galway city.

ANTIQUITIES

Kilmacduagh Churches and Round Tower (20 K5): one of Connacht's greater early monasteries, dating from c.AD 600. Founded by St Colman Mac Duagh and created a diocese in the 12th century. Remains include several churches, including a cathedral, Church of St John the Baptist, 'Glebe House', O'Heynes Church and St Mary's Church. The fine 11th-12th century round tower inclines from the perpendicular.

Ardamullivan Castle (20 K6): a 16th century O'Shaughnessy stronghold with some interesting windows.

Fiddaun Castle (20 K6): situated near Gort, this well-preserved 16th century O'Shaughnessy castle features an unusually planned bawn with an outer bawn of which the gatehouse remains.

Drumacoo Church (20 J4): dedicated to St Sorney, part of this church may date from the 8th or 10th century. The south doorway is a minor masterpiece of the Connacht transitional style.
Kiltiernan Church (20 K4): remains of an 8th century church with a chancel of later date. Site surrounded by circular enclosure.
Kiltartan (20 K5): a simple structure incorporating primitive, transitional and late Gothic features with a 15th century altar in the chancel.
Portumna Castle (21 D5): this castle of the Clanrickarde Earls dates from 1609. Damaged by fire in 1826, but now being restored, the Castle has several outstanding features.
Portumna Priory (21 D5): originally Cistercian, this Priory dates from 1254, having been rebuilt in the 15th century by the Dominicans.
Derryhiveny Castle (21 D5): erected by Donal O'Madden in 1693.
Clonfert Cathedral (21 E3): St Brendan the Navigator founded a monastery in Clonfert in AD 563. The Cathedral doorway dates from c.1160 and is one of the glories of Irish Romanesque.
Loughrea Carmelite Monastery (21 B4): Richard de Burgo founded this monastery in 1300. Contains tombs of old families of Loughrea.
The Turoe Stone (2 B3): this remarkable pillar stone dates from the first century. It is decorated with patterns of Celtic scrollwork.
Ballinasloe Castle (21 D2): built by the O'Kellys in the 14th century.
Kilconnell Franciscan Friary (21 C2): William O'Kelly founded this Friary in 1353. Buildings consist of church with nave, choir, south transept and aisle and some domestic buildings.
Athenry Castle (21 A3): built in the early 13th century by Meiler de Bermingham. The original surrounding bawn wall with two corner towers remains; the gables are a later addition.
Dominican Priory of Saints Peter and Paul, Athenry (21 A3): founded in 1241 and accidentally burnt in 1423 but later rebuilt. The Priory was restored between 1638 and 1644. Suffered greatly during Cromwellian wars.
Market Cross, Athenry (21 A3): carved base and head of a late 15th century 'lantern' or 'tabernacle' cross.
Claregalway Abbey and Castle (20 J2): Claregalway Franciscan Friary was built in 1252 by John de Cogan. The tower was added c.1433. Some interesting tombstones. The Castle, standing at the bridge over the river Clare, is 15th century.
Church of St Mary, Tuam (14 K7): built between 1861 and 1878 this Church incoporates the late 12th century chancel with its magnificent windows and arch. The 14th century chapter house adjoins the building.
Tuam Cross (14 K7): decorated 12th century cross.
Kilbennan Church and Round Tower (14 K7): a ruined round tower and fragmentary church mark the site of a foundation by St Benignus.
Cistercian Abbey, Abbeyknockmoy (21 A1): ruins of abbey founded in 1190, including a tower from the 13th century.
Dunmore Augustinian Abbey (15 A6): ruins of a small friary of Augustinian hermits, founded in 1425. Interesting doorway and tower.
De Birmingham Castle, near Dunmore (15 A6): strong 13th century structure, possibly occupying site of Turloch O'Connor's fort.
Ross Abbey, Headford (20 H1): well-preserved ecclesiastical remains, founded in 1357 for the Franciscans and enlarged during the 15th century.
Aughnanure Castle (20 G1): a restored 15th century O'Flaherty stronghold, standing on a rock island surrounded by a stream.
Inchagoill, Lough Corrib (20 G1): Early Christian remains on this picturesque island include the 5th century St Patrick's Church, Teampall na Naomh and some inscribed stones.
Ballykine Castle (14 G7): situated near Clonbur village, this little castle has some unusual architectural features.
Aran Islands - Inishmore Kilronan (19 D5), **Inishmaan** School (19 E5) **and Inisheer** Fort (19 E5): on these islands there are so many individual antiquities to be seen that it would not be possible to list them in full. They include churches, pillar-stones, ring forts, castles and ancient wells. The most outstanding of all is Dun Aonghus, a large stone fort covering 11 acres.
St McDara's Church and Grave (19 C3): situated on McDara's Island off Carna. The island has the remains of a small church with a holy well and three pilgrimage 'stations'.
Collegiate Church of St Nicholas, Galway (20 H3): erected in 1320, the shell of the original church is incorporated in the present structure. Tradition holds that Columbus worshipped here before setting out on his famous voyage. Some interesting carvings and relics.
Franciscan Abbey, Galway (20 H3): built in 1826 on site of a 13th century friary. 17th century gravestones at rear.
Lynch Memorial, Galway (20 H3): a marble tablet over a doorway near the Church of St Nicholas, bearing an inscription about the reputed execution by James Lynch FitzStephen of his son Walter.
Lynch's Castle, Galway (20 H3): originally an early 16th century tower-house, now housing a bank. Features include some interesting coats of arms.
Browne Doorway, Galway (20 H3): at the entrance to the John F. Kennedy Memorial Park, this doorway was removed from the Browne mansion in Upper Abbeygate Street.
Spanish Arch, Galway (20 H3): erected in 1594 to protect the quay where Spanish ships unloaded.

HOUSES, CASTLES AND GARDENS

Thoor Ballylee (20 K5): a 16th century tower-house, situated at Gort. Former summer home of the poet W.B. Yeats.
Dunguaire Castle (20 J4): stands on the south shore of Galway Bay at Kinvara. Bridges 1,300 years of Irish history. The Castle stands on the site of the 7th century stronghold of the Connacht kings.

UNIVERSITY

University College, Galway (20 H3): founded in 1845, this Tudor-style building was designed by Joseph D. Keane. Contains Galway municipal records from 1485 to 1818 and many rare books. Became a constituent college of the National University in 1908.

LITERARY ASSOCIATIONS

Several notable figures of Irish literature lived around Gort, including W.B. Yeats, Lady Gregory, Edward Martyn and Count Florimond de Basterot.
Doorus House, situated near Kinvara, (now a youth hostel) has associations with the same literary circle.
Killeenan Church near Craughwell is the burial place of the famous blind Mayo poet, Raftery.
The Aran Islands inspired the work of John Millington Synge as well as producing two notable native writers, Liam O'Flaherty and Máirtín O Direáin.
The 17th century historian Ruairi O'Flaherty was born near Furbo.
Spiddal was the birthplace of Irish language prose writer Máirtín Ó Cadhain. Padraic Pearse's cottage, now a national monument, is at Rosmuck. Renvyle House (now a hotel) was once the summer residence of writer-physician Oliver St John Gogarty.

MUSEUMS

Clonfert Museum (21 E3): objects of ecclesiastical, historical and folklore interest. Located in surviving gateway of the town.
Aughrim Heritage Centre (21 C3): mementoes of the Battle of Aughrim (1691) as well as household utensils, axes and archaelogical finds.
Mill Museum, Tuam (14 K7): first industrial museum in the West of Ireland.
Galway City Museum (20 H3): located at the Spanish Arch, this museum contains a cross section of material relating to life in Galway since the city's foundation.

TOURING AREA 7

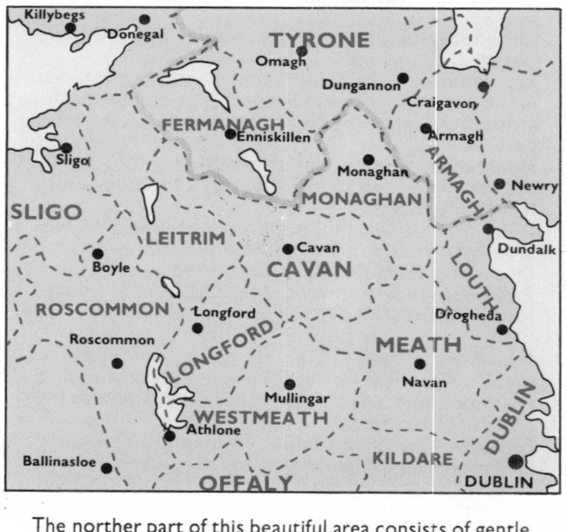

The norther part of this beautiful area consists of gentle coastal scenery combined with the mountains and hills of Co. Sligo and north Leitrim. The single most distinctive feature is the flat-topped Benbulben, north of Sligo town. This curious-looking mountain seems to be visible all over the region. Its strange haunting beauty never fails to intrigue the visitor. For the poet W.B. Yeats it became an object of great devotion, being situated in the centre of what is generally referred to as the Yeats Country.
Lakes are an important part of Area 7. Among the larger lakes are Lough Melvin to the north; the enchanting Lough Gill outside Sligo; Lough Key with its adjoining forest park near Boyle; and Lough Allen, the first of the great lakes of the river Shannon. The centre of the area is a cluster of smaller lakes noted the the quality of their fishing.
River cruising is an important tourist attraction, with a large well-equipped marina at Carrick-on-Shannon.
The southern section of this area is mainly a level plain of bogland and river meadow relieved by low hills and tiny lakes. There is no shortage of interesting towns and sleepy villages to visit, including Roscommon town, Boyle, Castlerea, Strokestown, Elphin and Ballaghaderreen.
All points within the area may be reached from Sligo town.

ANTIQUITIES

Sligo Abbey (7 B6): founded for the Dominicans in 1252 by Maurice Fitzgerald. Provides some outstanding examples of stone carving as well as interesting and well-preserved tombs.
Carrowmore (7 B6): here, 2 miles (3 km) from Sligo, are dolmens, stone circles and cairns with sepulchral monuments bearing carvings thought to date from the Bronze Age. The huge cairn, Maeve's Mound, is about 2 miles (3 km) away.
Drumcliff (7 B5): interesting ancient cross by the roadside, including Adam and Eve panel. Also lower part of round tower. Nearby is the grave of W.B. Yeats.
Creevykeel Court Cairn (7 C4): this is a magnificent example of a megalithic chamber tomb. A 1935 excavation resulted in several significant finds.
Ballymote Castle and Friary (15 B1): the Castle was built c.1300 by Richard de Burgo. Originally a well-defended fortress with six towers intact. The small Franciscan Third Order friary has an interesting east window.
Carrowkeel Passage Grave Cemetery (15 C1): this 4,000-year-old cemetery, with its fourteen cairns, is about 5 miles (8 km) from Ballymote.
Heapstown Passage Grave (15 C1): the great Heapstown cairn is located near Riverstown. Nearby is the Labby Rock, an enormous portal dolmen dating back about 4,500 years.
Kilcoo Monastery (7 E5): slight remains with a cross-inscribed gravestone.
Hamilton Castle, Dromahair (7 D6): built between 1634 and 1638; originally heavily fortified. Proved impregnable during 1641 war.
Parke's Castle (7 C6): this ruined Plantation castle with its large bawn in 5 miles (8 km) east of Sligo on the east shore of Lough Gill.
Creevelea Abbey, Dromahair (7 C6): founded in 1508 by Margaret, wife of Owen O'Rourke. Piece of notable carving portrays St Francis preaching to birds.
Tullaghan Cross (2 C4): Tullaghan is on the main Sligo-Bundoran road. Cross dates from the 9th or 10th century.
Roscommon Abbey (15 D6): remains of the church of a Dominican friary founded by King Felim O'Connor whose tomb is in the chancel.
Black Pig's Dyke (7 E5): ancient earthworks boundary dividing Ulster from Connacht. Remains can be seen in several townlands, including Kiltyclogher.
Roscommon Castle (15 D6): dating from 1269, this splendid Castle changed hands many times during its history. Covers large quadrangular area. Towers at each angle with two extra towers protecting gateway.
Fuerty Churchyard (15 D6): two early gravestones mark the site of a Patrician foundation.
Boyle Abbey (15 D2): founded in 1161 by Abbot Maurice O'Duffy, being daughter house of Mellifont. Well-preserved ruins include cruciform church with lofty tower.
Dromanone Portal Dolmen (15 C2): situated near Boyle, it is one of Ireland's largest dolmens.
Ballintober Castle (15 C5): formerly the chief seat of the O'Connors of Connacht after the Anglo-Norman invasion of Ireland. Built c.1300.

FOREST PARKS AND GARDENS

For full details see 'The Open Forest', a publication available from all tourist information offices.

HOUSES, CASTLES AND GARDENS

Lisadell House (7 B5): situated near Drumcliff, Co. Sligo. Former home of Eva Gore-Booth and Constance Markievicz. Still home of Gore-Booth family.
Clonalis House (15 B4): home of O'Conor Don. Located at Castlerea, Co. Roscommon. 19th century mansion in well-maintained parkland. Collection of Irish manuscripts, documents and books, also furniture and paintings. Woodland garden and walk.

Cloonusker 21 B7
Cloonycarney 6 J6
Cloonymorris 21 C3
Cloonyquin/Cluain Uí Choinn 15 D4
Closh 22 H6
Clough/An Chloch 10 K5
Cloyne/Cluain 34 H5
Coachford/Áth an Chóiste 33 C4
Coagh/An Cuach 9 D2
Coalbrook/Glaise an Ghuail 28 K3
Coalisland/Oileán an Ghuail 9 D3
Coan/An Cuan 29 CI
Cobh/An Cóbh 34 G5
Caddy 4 F7
Colbinstown/Baile Choilbín 23 D6
Colehill/Cnoc na Góla 16 H6
Coleraine/Cúil Raithin 3 D3
Colestown 30 G6
Collinstown/Baile na gCailleach 17 A6
Collon/Collan 17 E4
Collooney/Cúil Mhuine 7 B7
Colman 28 J5
Colmanstown/Baile Uí Chlúmháin 21 B2
Colp 18 G5
Comber/An Comar 12 H3
Commaun 28 G2
Commons, Co Cork 33 C5
Commons/Na Coimíní 29 A3
  Co Tipperary/Tiobraid Árann
Cong/Conga 14 G7
Conlig/An Choinleic 12 J2
Conna/Conaithe 34 H2
Connolly/Fíoch Rua 26 JI
Connonagh 36 F5
Convoy/Conmhaigh 2 H6
Cookstown/An Chorr Chríochach 9 D2
Cool 34 JI
Coolagary 23 A3
Coolaney/Cúil Áine 7 B7
Coolanheen 34 K2
Coolattin 30 H2
Coolbaun/An Cúl Bán 21 D6
Coolbaun/An Cúl Bán 29 CI
Coolboy, Co Tipperary 28 F7
Coolboy/An Cúl Buí 30 H2
  Co Wicklow/Cill Mhantáin
Coolderry/Cúl Doire 22 G6
Coole/An Chuil 16 K5
Coole Abbey 34 G2
Coolea/Cúil Aodha 34 F2
Coolgrange 29 C3
Coolgreany/Cúil Chréine 30 J2
Coolgreen 34 F3
Coolinny 34 F2
Coolmaghry 9 C3
Coolmeen/Cúil Mhín 26 J3
Coolnafarna 15 A5
Coolnagun 16 J5
Coolrain/Cúil Ruáin 22 H6
Coolroe 30 J4
Coolross 21 E5
Coolsallagh 34 F5
Coolshaghtena 15 E6
Coomleagh 32 K6
Coonagh 27 C3
Cooneen/An Cúinnín 8 K5
Cooraclare/Cuar an Chláir 26 H2
Coorleagh 29 D2
Coosane 35 C5
Cootehall/Uachtar Thire 15 E2
Cootehill/Muinchille 17 AI
Coralstown/Baile Mhic Cearúill 23 AI
Corbally, Co Clare 26 G2
Corbally/An Corrbhaile 6 J7
  Co Sligo/Sligeach
Corbay Upper 16 H5
Corbet Milltown 10 G5
Corclogh 5 B6
Corcullin 14 FI
Cordal/Cordal 32 JI
Cordarragh 14 F5
Corduff/An chorr Dubh 23 C3
Cork/Corcaigh 33 E4
Corkey/Corcaigh 4 F4
Corlea 16 F6

Corlee 14 J2
Cornafulla/Corr na Fola 21 E2
Cornanagh 14 H5
Corndarragh 22 J3
Corrandulla/Cor an Dola 20 J2
Correen 4 G6
Corrofin/Cora Finne 20 H7
  Co Clare/An Clár
Corrofin, Co Galway 20 KI
Cortown/An Baile Corr 17 C5
Corvoley 6 F7
Costelloe/Casla 19 E3
Coumduff 31 DI
Countygate 34 H2
Courthoyle 30 F6
Courtmatrix 27 A5
Courtown 30 J3
Cousane 32 K6
Coxtown 21 C3
Craan 30 H2
Craanford/Áth an Chorráin 30 H2
Crafield 24 G7
Cragroe 20 K7
Craig 3 A7
Craigavad/Creig an Bhada 10 KI
Craigavole 3 D5
Craigavon/Craigavon 10 F4
Craigs/Na Creaga 4 F6
Cranagh/An Chrannóg 3 A7
Crane 30 H4
Cranford/Creamhghort 2 G3
Cranny/An Chrannaigh 26 J2
  Co Clare/An Clár
Cranny 9 DI
  Co Londonderry/Doire
Cratloe/An Chreatalach 27 B2
Craughwell/Creachmhaoil 21 A3
Crawfordsburn/Sruth Chráfard 10 KI
Crazy Corner 16 K7
Creagh, Co Cork 35 D5
Creagh/Créach 8 J5
  Co Fermanagh/Fear Manach
Creaghanroe/Crícheán Rua 9 D7
Crecora/Craobh Chomhartha 27 C4
Creegh/An Chríoch 26 H2
Creeslough/An Craoslach 2 F3
Creevagh 6 G6
Creeves 27 A4
Cregg, Co Clare 20 H4
Cregg, Co Cork 36 F5
Creggan, Co Armagh 17 EI
Creggan, Co Ofaly 22 F3
Creggan/An Creagán 9 B2
  Co Tyrone/Tír Eoghain
Cregganbaun/An Creagán Bán 13 D5
Creggs/Na Creaga 15 C6
Crilly/Crithligh 9 B4
Crindle 3 B4
Crinkill/Crionchoill 22 F5
Croaghrimbeg 14 F5
Crockets Town 6 H7
Croghan/Cruachán 22 K2
  Co Offaly/Uíbh Fhailí
Croghan/Cruachán 15 D3
  Co Roscommon/Ros Coman
Cromane/An Cromán 31 E2
Cromlin 16 GI
Crookedwood/Tigh Munna 16 K6
Crookhaven/An Cruachán 35 B6
Crookstown/An Baile Gallda 33 C5
  Co Cork/Corcaigh
Crookstown, Co Kildare 23 D6
Croom/Cromadh 27 C4
Cross Barry/Croisan Bharraigh 33 D5
Cross Keys/Carraig an Tobair 16 K3
  Co Cavan/An Cabhán
Cross Keys, Co Meath 17 A5
Cross Keys, Co Meath 17 E7
Cross Mahon 33 C6
Cross Roads/Na Croisbhealaí 2 G7
Cross/An Chrois 25 E3
  Co Clare/An Clar
Cross, Co Waterford 34 K3
Crossabeg/Na Crosa Beaga 30 H6
Crossakeel/Crosa Caoil 17 B5

Crossboyne 14 J5
Crossconnell 21 D3
Crossdoney/Cros Domhnaigh 16 J2
Crossea 16 H6
Crosserlough/Crois ar Loch 16 K3
Crossgar/An chrois Ghearr 10 K4
Crossgare 3 D4
Crosshaven/Bun an Tábhairne 34 F5
Crosskeys/Na hEochracha 23 B5
Crossmaglen/Crois Mhic Lionnáin 17 EI
Crossmolina/Crois Mhaoilíona 14 GI
Crossna 15 D2
Crosspatrick/Crois Phádraig 28 K2
  Co Kilkenny/Cill Chainnigh
Crosspatrick, Co Wicklow 30 H2
Crosswell 15 C6
Crowbally 34 H4
Crumlin/Cromghlinn 10 G2
Crumpane 31 E6
Crusheen/Croisín 20 K7
Crutt 29 CI
Cuilkillew 14 G2
Culcavy 10 H4
Culdaff/Cúil Dabhcha 3 A2
Cullahill/An Chúlchoill 29 AI
Cullane 27 E6
Cullaville/Baile Mhic Cullach 17 DI
Culleen 27 B2
Culleens/Na Coillíní 6 J7
Cullen/Cuillin 33 A2
  Co Cork/Corcaigh
Cullen/Cuilleann 28 F4
  Co Tipperary/Tiobraid Árann
Cullenagh 27 E7
Cullenstown 36 GI
Cullin 14 J2
Cullinane 4 H5
Cullybackey/Coill na Baice 4 F6
Cullyhanna/Coilleach Eanach 9 E7
Culnady/Cúil Chnáidí 3 D6
Cultra 10 K2
Currabeha/An Chorr Bheithe 34 H2
Curracloe/Currach Cló 30 H6
Curraclogh 33 B5
Curragh/An Currach 34 K4
Curragh West/An Currach Thiar 15 A6
Curragha 18 F7
Curraghalicky 33 A7
Curraghboy/An Currach Buí 21 EI
Curraghlawn 30 HI
Curraghmore 27 EI
Curraghroe/An Currach Rua 15 E5
Curraglass/Cora Chlas 34 H2
Curragunneen/Currach Guinín 22 G7
Curran/An Corrán 3 D7
Curranavilla 20 F3
Currans 32 HI
Curreeny/Na Coirríní 28 G2
Currow/Corra 32 HI
Curry/An Choraidh 14 K2
Curryglass 32 F7
Cushendall/Bun Abhann Dalla 4 H4
Cushendun/Bun Abhann Duinne 4 H3
Cushina 23 A4

D

Daingean/An Daingean 22 K3
Damastown 18 G7
Damhead 3 D4
Danesfort/Dún Feart 16 G5
Dangan 34 H3
Dangandargan 28 H5
Darkley/Dearclaigh 9 D6
Darragh/An Darach 26 KI
Davidstown/Baile Dháith 30 G5
Deereenauliff 31 E5
Deerpark/Páirc na bhFia 14 H7
Delgany/Deilgne 24 H4
Delvin/Dealbhna 17 B6
Dernagree/Doire na Graí 33 A2
Derradda/Doire Fhada 16 GI
Derreen, Co Clare 20 F7
Derreen, Co Kerry 31 C4

Derreen/An Doirín 14 F2
  Co Mayo/Maigh Eo
Derreenacarrin 32 G6
Derreenard 35 D5
Derreeny 32 F7
Derries, Co Offaly 23 B3
Derries, Co Offaly 22 H3
Derrineel 21 E2
Derryadd/Doire Fhada 10 F3
Derrybeg/Doirí Beaga I D4
Derryboy/Doire Buí 12 H4
Derrybrien/Daraidh Braoin 21 A5
Derrycanan 15 E5
Derryclogh 32 K7
Derrycon 22 J5
Derrycooly 22 H3
Derrydolney 22 G4
Derryfada 28 K2
Derryfineen 32 K4
Derrygareen 27 E2
Derrygile 22 K5
Derrygolan 22 J2
Derrygonnelly/Doire Ó gConaíle 8 G4
Derrygowna 16 F6
Derrygrath 28 J6
Derrygrogan 22 K3
Derrykeighan 3 E3
Derrylahan 21 E2
Derryloughaun 20 G3
Derrylin/Doire Loinn 8 H7
Derryloughlin 32 F5
Derrymore 25 E7
Derrynoose/Doire Núis 9 D6
Derryrush 19 D2
Derrywode 15 B5
Dervock/Dearbhóg 3 E3
Desert 34 G3
Desertmartin/Díseart Mhártain 3 D7
Devenish/Daimhinis 8 H5
Dingle/An Daingean 31 CI
Doagh/Dumhach 10 HI
Dolla/An Doladh 28 FI
Dollingstown 10 G4
Dollymount/Cnocán Doirinne 24 H2
Donabate/Domhnach Bat 18 H7
Donacarney 18 G5
Donadea 23 D2
Donagh 8 J6
Donaghadee/Domhnach Daoi 12 J2
Donaghcloney/Domhnach Cluana 10 G4
Donaghmore/Domhnach Mór 22 H7
  Co Laois/Laois
Donaghmore, Co Meath 18 F7
Donaghmore/Domhnach Mór 9 C3
  Co Tyrone/Tír Eoghain
Donaghpatrick/Domhnach Phádraig 17 D5
Donard, Co Wexford 29 E5
Donard/Dún Ard 23 E6
  Co Wicklow/Cill Mhantáin
Donaskeagh 28 G4
Donegal/Dún na nGall 7 E2
Doneraile/Dún ar Aill 33 DI
Donohill/Dún Eochaille 28 G4
Donore/Dún Uabhair 18 F5
Donoughmore/Domhnach Mór 33 C3
Dooagh/Dumha Acha 13 B2
Doocastle/Caisleán an Dumha 15 A2
Doocharry/An Dúchoraidh I D6
Dooega/Dumha Éige 13 B3
Dooghbeg 13 C3
Doohat/Dúháite 17 AI
Doohooma/Dumha Thuama 13 CI
Doolieve 33 E6
Doon, Co Galway 21 C2
Doon/Dún 28 F3
  Co Limerick/Luimneach
Doon, Co Tipperary 34 HI
Doonaha/Dún Átha 26 F3
Doonbeg/An Dún Beag 26 G2
Doonmanagh 31 D2
Doornane 29 C7
Dooyork 13 CI
Dough 35 A6
Doughiska 20 J3
Douglas/Dúglas 33 E5

Dovea/*An Dubhfhéith* 28 H2
Dowling 29 B6
Downhill/ *Dún Bó* 3 C3
Downing 34 FI
Downpatrick/*Dún Pádraig* 12 H5
Dowra/*An Damhsraith* 7 E7
Drangan/*Drongan* 28 K4
Draperstown/*Baile na Croise* 3 C7
Dreen 3 B6
Dreenagh 25 D5
Drehidasillagh 25 E7
Driminidy 32 K7
Drimmo 22 J6
Drimoleague/*Drom Dhá Liag* 32 K7
Drinagh/*Draighneagh* 32 K7
  Co Cork/*Corcaigh*
Drinagh, Co Galway 19 BI
Drinagh, Co Roscommon 16 F5
Drinagh, Co Wexford 30 H7
Drinaghan 6 J6
Dring/*Droing* 16 J4
Dripsey/*An Druipseach* 33 C4
Drogheda/*Droichead Átha* 18 F5
Drom, Co Kerry 25 C7
Drom/*An Drom* 28 H2
  Co Tipperary/*Tiobraid Árann*
Dromahair/*Droim dhá Thiar* 7 D6
Dromara/*Droim Bearach* 10 H5
Dromaragh 31 D4
Dromboy South 33 E3
Dromcolliher 27 A6
Dromcunnig 26 F6
Dromgariff 33 E3
Dromin, Co Limerick 27 D5
Dromin/*Droim Ing* 18 F4
  Co Louth/*Lú*
Dromina/*Drom Aidhne* 27 B7
Dromineer/*Drom Inbhir* 21 D7
Dromiskin/*Droim Ineasclainn* 18 F3
Drommahane/*Droim Átháin* 33 D2
Dromnea 35 B5
Dromod/*Dromad* 16 F3
Dromore West/*An Droim Mór Thiar* 6 K6
Dromore/*Droim Mór* 10 H4
  Co Down/*An Dún*
Dromore/*An Droim Mór* 8 J3
  Co Tyrone/*Tír Eoghain*
Dromore, Co Waterford 34 K2
Dromtrasna 26 J6
Drum/*An Droim* 17 AI
  Co Monaghan/*Muineachán*
Drum, Co Roscommon 21 E2
Drumahoe 2 K5
Drumaness/*Droim an Easa* 12 G5
Drumanure 26 KI
Drumatober 21 C4
Drumbane/*An Drom Bán* 28 H3
Drumbaun 27 E2
Drumbeg 10 J3
Drumbo 10 J3
Drumcar/*Droim Chora* 18 F3
Drumcharley 21 A7
Drumcliff, Co Clare 20 J7
Drumcliff/*Droim Chliabh* 7 B5
  Co Sligo/*Sligeach*
Drumcondra/*Droim Conrach* 17 D3
Drumcree/*Droim Cria* 17 A6
Drumfin/*Droim Fionn* 7 C7
Drumfree/*Droim Fraoigh* 2 J3
Drumgriftin 20 J2
Drumkeary 21 B5
Drumkeeran/*Droim Caorthainn* 7 E7
Drumlea/*Droim Léith* 16 G2
Drumlish/*Droim Lis* 16 G4
Drumlosh 22 F2
Drummin/*An Dromainn* 26 HI
Drummullin/*Droim Ailí* 15 E4
Drumna 16 G2
Drumnagreagh Port 4 J5
Drumnakilly/*Droim na Coille* 9 A2
Drumoghill 2 H6
Drumone 17 A5
Drumquin/*Droim Caoin* 8 J2
Drumraney/*Droim Raithne* 22 GI
Drumree/*Droim Rí* 17 E7

Drumroe 34 J2
Drumshanbo/*Droim Seanbhó* 15 EI
Drumskinny/*Droim Scine* 8 G3
Drumsna/*Droim ar Snámh* 15 E3
Drumsurn/*Droim Sorn* 3 C5
Duagh/*Dubháth* 26 H5
Dually 28 J4
Dublin/*Baile Átha Cliath* 24 G2
Duggarry 21 E2
Duleek/*Damhliag* 18 F6
Dumfea 29 E3
Dunadry/*Dún Eadradh* 10 HI
Dunany/*Dún Áine* 18 G3
Dunbarton 10 F5
Dunbell 29 C3
Dunboyne/*Dún Búinne* 24 FI
Dunbyrne 23 C3
Duncannon/*Dún Canann* 36 FI
Duncormick/*Dún Chormaic* 36 HI
Dundalk/*Dún Dealgan* 18 F2
Dunderrow/*Dún Darú* 33 D6
Dunderry 17 D6
Dundian 9 B5
Dundonald/*Dún Dónaill* 10 K2
Dundoogan 21 C2
Dundrod/*Dún dTrod* 10 H2
Dundrum/*Dún Droma* 10 K6
  Co Down/*An Dún*
Dundrum/*Dún Droma* 24 G3
  Co Dublin/*Baile Átha Cliath*
Dundrum/*Dún Droma* 28 G4
  Co Tipperary/*Tiobraid Árann*
Dunfanaghy/*Dún Fionnachaidh* 2 F3
Dungannon/*Dún Geanainn* 9 C3
Dunganstown 29 D6
Dungarvan/*Dún Garbháin* 29 D4
  Co Kilkenny/*Cill Chainnigh*
Dungarvan/*Dún Garbhán* 35 A2
  Co Waterford/*Port Láirge*
Dungiven/*Dún Geimhin* 3 B6
Dunglow/*An Clochán Liath* 1 C5
Dungourney/*Dún Guairne* 34 H4
Dunhill 35 DI
Duniry 21 C5
Dunkerrin/*Dún Cairin* 22 F7
Dunkineely/*Dún Cionnaola* 7 C2
Dunkitt 29 C7
Dunlavin/*Dún Luáin* 23 D5
Dunleary 24 H3
Dunleer/*Dún Léire* 18 F4
Dunlewy/*Dún Lúiche* 1 E5
Dunloy/*Dún Lathaí* 4 F5
Dunmanus 35 B5
Dunmanway/*Dún Mánmhaí* 33 A6
Dunmoon 34 J3
Dunmore/*Dún Mór* 15 A6
Dunmore East/*Dún Mór* 35 EI
Dunmurry/*Dún Muirígh* 10 H3
Dunnamaggan/*Dún Iomagáin* 29 B5
Dunnamanagh/*Dún na Manach* 2 K6
Dunnamore/*Domhnach Mór* 9 BI
Dunningstown 29 B3
Dunquin/*Dún Chaoin* 31 BI
Dunseverick/*Dún Sobhairce* 3 E2
Dunshaughlin/*Dún Seachlainn* 17 E7
Durrow/*Darú* 29 BI
Durrus/*Dúras* 32 H7
Dún Laoghaire 24 H3
Dyan/*An Daighean* 9 C5
Dysart/*An Díseart* 22 JI

E

Eadestown 23 E4
Earlshill 28 K3
Easky/*Iaskaigh* 6 J6
Eden/*An tEadan* 12 HI
Edenderry/*Éadan Doire* 23 B?
Ederney/*Eadarnaidh* 8 H3
Edgeworthstown/*Meathas Troim* 16 H5
Eglinton/*An Mhagh* 3 A4
Eglish/*An Eaglais* 9 C4
Eighter/*Iochtar* 17 A4
Ellistrin/*Eileastran* 2 G5
Elphin/*Ail Finn* 15 D4

Elton/*Eiltiún* 27 D5
Emlagh Cross Roads 21 A4
Emly/*Imleach* 27 E5
Emmoo 15 E6
Emo/*Ioma* 23 A5
Emyvale/*Scairbh na gCaorach* 9 B5
Ennis/*Inis* 27 AI
Enniscorthy/*Inis Córthaidh* 30 G4
Enniskean/*Inis Céin* 33 B6
Enniskerry/*Áth an Sceire* 24 H4
Enniskillen/*Inis Ceithleann* 8 H5
Ennistimon/*Inis Díomáin* 20 G7
Erra 16 F5
Errill/*Eiréil* 28 KI
Esker/*An Eiscir* 21 A3
Esker South 16 G4
Eskragh/*Eiscreach* 9 A4
Eustace 23 E4
Eyeries/*Na hAoraí* 31 E6
Eyrecourt/*Dún an Uchta* 21 E4

F

Faha Glen 35 BI
Fahaduff 26 H7
Fahamore 25 D7
Fahan/*Fathain* 2 J4
  Co Donegal/*Dun na nGall*
Fahan, Co Kerry 31 B2
Fahanasoodry 27 E6
Fahy, Co Galway 21 C3
Fahy, Co Galway 21 D4
Fair Green 20 J7
Fairfield 22 GI
Fairymount/*Mullach na Sí* 15 B4
Falcarragh/*An Fál Carrach* 1 E3
Fanore 20 G5
Farahy 33 EI
Fardrum/*Fardroim* 22 F2
Farmer's Bridge 26 F7
Farnagh 22 G2
Farnaght 16 G3
Farnanes/*Na Fearnáin* 32 K6
Farnoge 29 D6
Farran/*An Fearann* 33 C5
Farranfore/*An Fearann Fuar* 32 HI
Fauna 23 E6
Feakle/*An Fhiacail* 21 A7
Fedamore/*Feadamair* 27 C4
Feeard 25 E3
Feenagh, Co Clare 20 H5
Feenagh/*Fíonach* 27 B6
  Co Limerick/*Luimneach*
Feeny/*Na Fineadha* 3 B6
Fenagh/*Fionnmhach* 16 G2
Fenit/*An Fhianait* 25 E7
Fennagh/*Fionnmhach* 29 E2
Fennor/*Fionnúir* 35 DI
  Co Waterford/*Port Láirge*
Fennor, Co Westmeath 17 A7
Feohanagh, Co Kerry 31 BI
Feohanagh/*An Fheothanach* 27 A6
  Co Limerick/*Luimneach*
Feoramore 32 G5
Ferbane/*An Féar Bán* 22 G3
Fermoy/*Mainistir Fhear Maí* 34 G2
Ferns/*Fearna* 30 H3
Ferry Bridge 27 B3
Ferrybank/*Portan Chalaidh* 30 KI
Fethard/*Fiodh Ard* 28 K5
  Co Tipperary/*Tiobraid Árann*
Fethard/*Fiodh Ard* 36 FI
  Co Wexford/*Loch Garman*
Fews 35 BI
Fiddane 27 E2
Fiddown/*Fiodh Dúin* 29 B6
Fieries 32 HI
Figlash 29 A6
Finavarra 20 H4
Finnea/*Fiodh an Átha* 16 K4
Finnis 10 H5
Finny/*Fionnaithe* 14 F7
Fintona/*Fionntamhnach* 8 K3
Fintown/*Baile na Finne* 1 E6
Finuge/*Fionnúig* 26 G5

Finvoy/*An Fhionnbhoith* 3 E5
Firkeel 31 D7
Firmount 34 G3
Fisherstreet 20 F6
Five Corners 4 H7
Fivealley/*An Chúirt* 22 G4
Fivemilebourne/*Abhainn an Chartúin* 7 C6
Fivemilebridge 33 E5
Fivemiletown/*Baile na Lorgan* 8 K5
Flagford 15 E3
Flagmount/*Leacain an Éadain* 21 A6
  Co Clare/*An Clár*
Flagmount, Co Kilkenny 29 D3
Flatfield 10 G3
Flemingstown 31 EI
Florence Court/*Mullach na Seangán* 8 H6
Flurrybridge 18 FI
Foilnamuck 35 C5
Fontstown 23 C5
Fordstown/*Baile Forda* 17 C6
Fore/*Baile Fhobhair* 17 A5
Forkill/*Foirceal* 18 FI
Formoyle, Co Clare 20 G5
Formoyle, Co Clare 26 KI
Formoyle, Co Mayo 13 C5
Fort Middle 27 B6
Fort William 21 E7
Forthill 16 F7
Foulksmill/*Muileann Fúca* 30 F7
Foulkstown 28 J4
Four Mile Ho/
  Teach na gCeithre Mhíle 15 D5
Four Roads/*Tigh Srathra* 15 D7
Fox Hill 14 F6
Foxfield/*Cnocán an Mhada Rua* 16 F2
Foxford/*Béal Easa* 14 H2
Foxhall 14 J6
Foynes/*Faing* 26 K3
Frankford 22 G4
Freemount/*Cillín an Chrónáin* 27 A7
Frenchpark/*Dún Gar* 15 C3
Freshford/*Achadh Úr* 29 B2
Freynestown 23 D6
Friarstown 27 C4
Frogmore 25 E7
Frosses/*Na Frosa* 7 DI
Fuerty 15 D6
Funshin More 20 J5
Furraleigh 35 BI
Furroor 26 J2
Furrow 28 F7

G

Gainestown 22 KI
Galbally/*An Gallbhaile* 27 E6
  Co Limerick/*Luimneach*
Galbally, Co Wexford 30 G6
Galbertstown 28 J3
Galgorm/*Galgorm* 4 F6
Gallagh 15 E6
Galmoy/*Gabhalmhaigh* 28 KI
Galtrim 17 D7
Galway/*Gaillimh* 20 J3
Gannavane 28 F3
Garadice/*Garairis* 23 DI
Garbally 21 D2
Garlow Cross/*Crois Chearla* 17 E6
Garnavilla 28 H6
Garr 23 A2
Garrane 33 A4
Garranereagh 33 B5
Garranlahan/*An Garrán Leathan* 15 A5
Garraun, Co Clare 26 G3
Garraun, Co Galway 21 C4
Garraun, Co Kerry 32 GI
Garravoone 29 B6
Garrettstown 23 D7
Garrison/*An Garastún* 7 E4
Garristown/*Baile Gháire* 18 F7
Garrycaheragh 34 H3
Garrycloonagh 14 GI
Garrycullen 30 F7
Garryduff 3 E4
Garryfine/*Garraí Phaghain* 27 C6

Garrymore	34	H4
Garrynafana	28	G1
Garryvoe	34	H5
Garvagh/*Garbhach*	16	F2
Co Leitrim/*Liatroim*		
Garvagh/*Garbhachadh*	3	D5
Co Londonderry/*Doire*		
Garvaghy/*Garbhachadh*	9	A3
Gattabaun/*An Geata Bán*	29	A2
Gawley's Gate/		
Geata Mhic Amhlai	10	F3
Gaybrook/*Baile Réamainn*	22	K1
Geashill/*Géisill*	22	K3
Geevagh/*An Ghaobhach*	15	D1
Geoghegan	22	J1
Georgestown	35	C1
Gerahies	32	H7
Gilford/*Áth Mhic Giolla*	10	F5
Glanalin	35	B5
Glandart	32	J7
Glandore/*Cuan Dor*	36	F5
Glanmire/*Gleann Maghair*	34	C2
Glanoe	26	G6
Glanroon	35	A5
Glantane/*An Gleanntán*	33	C2
Glanworth/*Gleannúir*	34	F1
Glarryford/*An tÁth Glárach*	4	F5
Glashabeg	31	B1
Glashaboy East	33	E3
Glashaboy North	33	E3
Glashananoon	26	H6
Glasleck/*Glasleic*	17	C2
Glaslough/*Glasloch*	9	C5
Glassan/*Glasán*	22	F1
Glassillaun	13	C3
Glastry	12	K3
Glebe	3	B3
Glen of Imail/		
Gleann Ó Máil	23	E6
Glen/*An Gleann*	2	G3
Co Donegal/*Dún na nGall*		
Glen, Co Londonderry	3	D6
Glenacroghery	34	H3
Glenade	7	C5
Glenagat	28	J6
Glenagort	14	F2
Glenahilty	21	E7
Glenamoy/*Gleann na Muaidhe*	5	D6
Glenard/*Gleann Aird*	35	A3
Glenariff/*Gleann Aireamh*	4	H4
Glenarm/*Gleann Arma*	4	J5
Glenavy/*Lann Abhaidh*	10	G2
Glenboy/*Gleann Buí*	7	E6
Glenbrien/*Gleann Bhriain*	30	H5
Glenbrohane	27	E6
Glencolumbkille/		
Gleann Cholm Cille	7	A1
Glencullen	24	G3
Glendalough/*Gleann dá Loch*	28	K7
Glendarragh	24	H5
Glenderry/*Gleann Doire*	25	E6
Glendowan/*Gleann Domhain*	2	F5
Glendree	20	K7
Glenduff	28	F7
Glenealy/*Gleann Fhaidhe*	24	H6
Glenedagh	6	F6
Gleneely/*Gleann Daoile*	3	A2
Glenfarne/*Gleann Fearna*	8	F6
Glengarriff/*An Gleann Garbh*	32	H6
Glengoura	34	H2
Glenhead	3	B5
Glenlara	5	B6
Glenmore, Co Clare	26	J2
Glenmore/*An Gleann Mór*	29	D6
Co Kilkenny/*Cill Chainnigh*		
Glennaknockane	26	J7
Glennamaddy/*Gleann na Madach*	15	B6
Glennascaul	20	J3
Glenoe	4	J7
Glenough Lower	28	G3
Glenough Upper	28	G3
Glenshelane	34	K1
Glentane, Co Cork	34	H3
Glentane, Co Galway	21	B1
Glenties/*Na Gleannta*	1	D7
Glentogher/*Gleann Tóchair*	2	K2
Glentrasna	19	E1
Glenvale	4	F5
Glenvar/*Gleann Bhairr*	2	H3
Glenville/		
Gleann an Phréacháin	34	F3
Glin/*An Gleann*	26	J4
Glinsk/*Glinsce*	19	C2
Glynn/*An Gleann*	4	K7
Co Antrim/*Aontroim*		
Glynn/*An Gleann*	29	E5
Co Wexford/*Loch Garman*		
Gneevgullia/*Gníomh go Leith*	32	K2
Golden/*An Gabhailín*	28	H5
Golden Ball	24	H3
Goleen/*An Góilín*	35	B6
Goold's Cross/*Crois an Ghúlaigh*	28	H4
Goresbridge/*An Droichead Nua*	29	D3
Gorey/*Guaire*	30	J3
Gormanston/*Baile Mhic Gormáin*	18	G6
Gormanstown	28	H7
Corrakyle	21	B6
Gort/*An Gort*	20	K5
Gortaclady	9	C2
Gortagowan	32	F5
Gortahork/*Gort an Choirce*	1	E3
Gortalough	28	H2
Gortarevan	21	E4
Gortaroo	34	J4
Gorteen/*Goirtín*	21	B2
Co Galway/*Gaillimh*		
Gorteen, Co Kilkenny	29	C1
Gorteen, Co Limerick	27	B6
Gorteen/*Goirtín*	15	B2
Co Sligo/*Sligeach*		
Gorteen, Co Waterford	35	A3
Gorteens	29	D7
Gorteeny/*Giortíní*	21	C6
Gortgarrift	31	E6
Gortgarrigan/*Gort Geargáin*	7	D6
Gortglass	32	J1
Gortin/*An Goirtín*	8	K1
Gortleatilla	5	E6
Gortletteragh	16	G3
Gortmore, Co Galway	19	E2
Gortmore, Co Mayo	6	G6
Gortnadeeve	15	C6
Gortnahaha	26	K3
Gortnahey	3	B5
Gortnahoo/*Gort na hUamha*	28	K3
Gortnahoughtee	32	K5
Gortnahurra	6	F7
Gortnaleaha	26	G7
Gortnamearacaun	20	K7
Gortnasillagh	15	C4
Gortreagh/*An Gort Riabhach*	9	C2
Gortrelig	32	F3
Gortskeagh	20	J5
Gowlaun	13	C6
Gowlin	29	E4
Gowran/*Gabhrán*	29	D3
Gracehill/*Baile Uí Chinnéide*	4	F6
Graigue/*An Ghráig*	34	F3
Graiguenamanagh/		
Gráig na Manach	29	E4
Granabeg	24	F5
Granard/*Granard*	16	J4
Graney	23	D7
Grange Beg, Co Kildare	23	C4
Grange Beg, Co Laois	22	H7
Grange Con/*Gráineach Choinn*	23	D6
Grange/*Gráinseach Chuffe*	29	B4
Co Kilkenny/*Cill Chainnigh*		
Grange, Co Kilkenny	29	C7
Grange, Co Offaly	23	B2
Grange/*An Ghráinseach*	7	B5
Co Sligo/*Sligeach*		
Grange/*An Ghráinsigh*	34	K3
Co Waterford/*Port Láirge*		
Grange, Co Wexford	36	H1
Grangebellew/		
Gráinseach an Dísirt	18	G4
Grangeford/*An Ghráinseach*	30	F1
Grangegeeth	17	E5
Grannagh	20	K4
Grant House	9	C4
Granville/*An Doire Mhin*	9	C3
Greenan/*An Grainán*	24	G7
Greenanstown/*Baile Uí Ghrianáin*	18	G6
Greencastle/*An Caisleán Nua*	3	B3
Co Donegal/*Dún na nGall*		
Greencastle/*Caisleán na hOireanaí*	18	H1
Co Down/*An Dún*		
Greencastle, Co Tyrone	9	A1
Greenisland/*Inis Glas*	10	J1
Greenland	34	J4
Grenagh/*Greanach*	33	D3
Greyabbey/*An Mhainistir Liath*	12	J3
Greygrove	26	J2
Greysteel	3	A4
Greysteel/*An Chloch Liath*	9	C4
Greystones/*Na Clocha Liatha*	24	H4
Griston	27	E6
Grogan	22	G2
Groomsport/		
Port an Ghialla Chruama	12	J1
Gulladuff	3	D7
Gullaun	32	K2
Gurteen/*Goirtín*	7	D5
Gusserane/*Ráth na gCosarán*	29	E7
Gweedore/*Gaoth Dobhair*	1	D4
Gweesalia/*Gaoth Sáile*	13	C1
Gyleen	34	G5

H

Hacketstown	23	E7
Halfway House/*Tigh Leath Slí*	35	E1
Hamiltonsbawn/*Bábhún Hamaltún*	9	E5
Hannahstown/*Baile Haine*	10	H2
Harristown	29	C6
Hays	17	E5
Headford/*Áth Cinn*	20	H1
Heathfield	33	E6
Heavenstown	30	G7
Heirhill	25	E5
Helen's Bay/*Cuan Héilin*	10	K1
Herbertstown/*Baile Hiobaird*	27	D4
High Street	22	F3
Hightown	34	G3
Hill of Down/*Cnoc an Dúin*	23	B1
Hill Street	15	E3
Hillhall	10	H3
Hillsborough/*Cromghlinn*	10	H4
Hilltown/*Baile Hill*	10	H7
Co Down/*An Dún*		
Hilltown, Co Wexford	30	H7
Hilltown, Co Wexford	30	F7
Hollyford/*Áth an Chuilinn*	28	G3
Hollyfort/*Ráth an Chuilinn*	30	J2
Hollymount, Co Galway	21	A5
Hollymount/*Maolla*	14	H6
Co Mayo/*Maigh Eo*		
Hollywood/*Cillín Chaoimhín*	23	E5
Holycross/*Baile na gCailleach*	27	D5
Co Limerick/*Luimneach*		
Holycross/*Mainstir na Croiche*	28	H3
Co Tipperary/*Tiobraid Árann*		
Holywell	8	F6
Holywood/*Ard Mhic Nasca*	10	K2
Horetown	30	H7
Horse and Jockey/*An Marcach*	28	J3
Horseleap/*Baile Átha an Urchair*	22	H2
Hospital/*An tOspidéal*	27	E5
Hough	28	H3
Howth/*Binn Éadair*	24	H2
Hugginstown	29	C5
Hurlers Cross	27	B2
Hyde Park	10	H1

I

Illaunstookagh	31	E2
Inagh/*Eigneagh*	20	H7
Inch, Co Cork	34	J3
Inch, Co Cork	34	G5
Inch, Co Kerry	31	E1
Inch, Co Tipperary	28	G3
Inch/*An Inis*	30	J2
Co Wexford/*Loch Garman*		
Inchbeg	29	B2
Inchigeelagh/*Inse Geimhleach*	33	A5
Inchinapallas	34	F1
Inchnamuck	28	G7
Inishannon	33	D6
Inishcrone/*Inis Crabhann*	6	H7
Inishrush	3	E6
Iniskeen/*Inis Caoin*	17	E2
Inistioge/*Inis Tíog*	29	D5
Innfield/*An Bóthar Buí*	23	C1
Inveran/*Indreabhan*	20	F3
Irishtown/*An Baile Gaelach*	14	K6
Irvinestown/*Baile an Irbhinigh*	8	H4

J

Jamestown, Co Laois	23	A5
Jamestown, Co Leitrim	15	E3
Jerrettspass/*Bealach Sheirit*	10	F6
Johnsfort	14	J3
Johnstown Bridge	23	C2
Johnstown/*Cill Sheanaigh*	34	F5
Co Cork/*Corcaigh*		
Johnstown/*Baile Sheáin*	29	A2
Co Kilkenny/*Cill Chainnigh*		
Johnstown, Co Meath	17	D6
Johnstown, Co Tipperary	23	E3
Johnstown, Co Wexford	30	F7
Johnstown, Co Wicklow	30	K1
Johnstown, Co Wicklow	30	J1
Johnstownbridge	16	F4
Johnswell/*Tobar Eoin*	29	C2
Jonesborough/*Baile an Chláir*	18	F1
Julianstown/*Baile Iuiliáin*	18	G5

K

Kanturk/*Ceann Toirc*	33	B1
Katesbridge/*Droichead Cháit*	10	H5
Keadew/*Céideadh*	15	E1
Keady/*An Céide*	9	D6
Kealkill/*An Chaolchoill*	32	J6
Kealvaugh	32	K5
Keeagh	20	G2
Keel/*An Caol*	13	B2
Keelnagore	31	D4
Keeloges	15	B6
Keenagh/*Caonagh*	16	G6
Co Longford/*An Longfort*		
Keenagh, Co Mayo	14	F1
Keenaunnagark	19	E3
Keereen	34	K2
Kells/*Ceanannas*	29	B4
Kells Connor/*Na Cealla*	4	G7
Kelshabeg	23	E7
Kenmare/*Neidín*	32	H4
Kentstown	17	E6
Kerloge	30	H7
Kesh/*An Cheis*	8	G3
Co Fermanagh/*Fear Manach*		
Kesh/*An Chéis*	15	C1
Co Sligo/*Sligeach*		
Keshcarrigan/*Ceis Charraigin*	16	F2
Kilaloe	27	E1
Kilbaha/*Cill Bheathach*	25	E4
Kilbane/*An choill Bhán*	27	D1
Kilbarry/*Cill Barra*	29	C7
Kilbeacanty	20	K5
Kilbeg	35	C1
Kilbeggan/*Cill Bheagáin*	22	J2
Kilbegnet	15	C6
Kilbeheny/*Coill Bheithne*	28	F7
Kilberry/*Cill Bhearaigh*	23	B6
Co Kildare/*Cill Dara*		
Kilberry, Co Meath	17	D5
Kilbrack	29	A7
Kilbreedy, Co Limerick	27	B4
Kilbreedy, Co Limerick	27	C6
Kilbreedy, Co Tipperary	28	H4
Kilbrickan	19	E2
Kilbrickane	28	J2
Kilbricken/*Cill Bhriocáin*	29	C7
Kilbride, Co Mayo	14	J3
Kilbride, Co Meath	17	C6

Kilbride/Cill Bhríde	24 F4	Kilkee/Cill Chaoi	26 F2
Co Wicklow/Cill Mhantáin		Kilkeel/Cill Chaoil	18 J1
Kilbride/Cill Bhríde	24 H7	Kilkelly/Cill Cheallaigh	14 K3
Co Wicklow/Cill Mhantáin		Co Mayo/Maigh Eo	
Kilbrien, Co Cork	34 F2	Kilkenny West	22 G1
Kilbrien, Co Waterford	35 A1	Kilkenny/Cill Chainnigh	29 C3
Kilbrin	33 C1	Co Kilkenny/Cill Chainnigh	
Kilbrittain/Cill Briotáin	33 D7	Kilkerran	33 D7
Kilcaimin	20 J3	Kilkerrin/Cill Choirín	15 B7
Kilcar/Cill Charthaigh	7 B2	Kilkieran/Cill Chiaráin	19 D2
Kilcarney	23 E7	Kilkilleen	35 D5
Kilcarroll	26 H3	Kilkinlea	26 J6
Kilcash	29 A6	Kilkishen/Cill Chisín	27 B1
Kilcashel	21 E2	Kill/An Chill	17 A2
Kilcavan	22 K4	Co Cavan/An Cabhán	
Kilchreest/Cill Chríost	21 A4	Kill/An Chill	23 E3
Kilclaran	21 A7	Co Kildare/Cill Dara	
Kilclief	12 J5	Kill/An Chill	35 C1
Kilcloher	25 E4	Co Waterford/Port Láirge	
Kilclonfert	22 K2	Killachonna	22 G1
Kilcock/Cill Choca	23 D2	Killaclug	27 E7
Kilcoe	35 D5	Killacolla	27 B6
Kilcogy/Cill Chóige	16 J4	Killadeas/Cill Chéile Dé	8 H4
Kilcohan	35 E1	Killaderry	21 C1
Kilcolgan/Cill Cholgáin	20 K4	Killadoon/Coill an Dúin	13 C5
Kilcolman, Co Cork	33 C6	Killadysert/Cill an Dísirt	26 K3
Kilcolman/Cill Cholmáin	26 K4	Killafeen	20 K6
Co Limerick/Luimneach		Killag	36 H1
Kilcolman, Co Waterford	35 A3	Killahaly	34 J2
Kilcomin	22 F6	Killala/Cill Ala	6 H7
Kilcommon/Cill Chuimín	28 G2	Killallon	17 B5
Co Tipperary/Tiobraid Árann		Killamery	29 A5
Kilcommon, Co Tipperary	28 H6	Killane	23 B2
Kilcon	6 G7	Killanena	21 A6
Kilconierin	21 A3	Killann/Cill Anna	30 F4
Kilconly/Cill Chonla	14 J7	Killard	26 G2
Kilconnell/Cill Chonaill	21 C2	Killare	22 H1
Kilconnor	27 D7	Killarga/Cill Fhearga	7 D6
Kilcoo/Cill Chua	10 H6	Killarney/Cill Airne	32 H2
Kilcoole/Cill Chomhghaill	24 H5	Killarone	20 G1
Kilcor	34 G2	Killaroo	22 H1
Kilcorkan	20 J6	Killashandra/	
Kilcormac/Cill Chormaic	22 G4	Cill na Seanrátha	16 J2
Kilcornan	27 B3	Killashee/Cill na Sí	16 F5
Kilcorney/Cill Coirne	33 B2	Killasser/Cill Lasrach	14 J2
Kilcotty/Cill Chota	30 H5	Killaun	22 G5
Kilcredan	34 J4	Killavally/Coill an Bhaile	14 F5
Kilcrohane/Cill Chrócháin	35 B5	Killavarilly	34 G2
Kilcronat	34 H3	Killavarrig	33 E3
Kilcullen/Cill Chuillin	23 D5	Killavil/Cill Fhábhail	15 B2
Kilcummin, Co Kerry	25 C7	Killavoher	15 A7
Kilcummin/Cill Chuimín	32 H2	Killavullen/Cill an Mhuilinn	33 E2
Co Kerry/Ciarraí		Killea, Co Donegal	2 J5
Kilcurly/Cill Choirle	18 F2	Killea, Co Leitrim	7 E5
Kilcurry/Cill an Churraigh	18 F1	Killea/Cill Shléibhe	28 H1
Kilcusnaun	26 H7	Co Tipperary/Tiobraid Árann	
Kildalkey/Cill Dealga	17 C7	Killea, Co Waterford	35 E1
Kildangan/Cill Daingin	23 B5	Killead/Cill Éad	10 G2
Kildare/Cill Dara	23 C4	Killeagh/Cill Ia	34 J4
Kildavin/Cill Damhain	30 F3	Killealy	10 G1
Kildermody	29 B7	Killeany	19 D5
Kildorrery/Cill Dairbhre	27 E7	Killedmond	29 E3
Kildress	9 C2	Killeedy	26 K6
Kilduffahoo	27 E3	Killeen, Co Galway	20 K6
Kildurrihy	31 B1	Killeen, Co Tipperary	22 F5
Kilfeakle	28 G5	Killeen, Co Tyrone	9 D3
Kilfearagh	26 F3	Killeenaran	20 J4
Kilfenora/Cill Fhionnúrach	20 G6	Killeenasteena	28 H5
Kilfinnane/Cill Fhíonáin	27 D6	Killeenavarra	20 J4
Kilfinny	27 B4	Killeeneenmore	20 K4
Kilflynn/Cill Flainn	26 F6	Killeenleagh	32 J7
Kilgarvan/Cill Gharbháin	32 J4	Killeens Cross	33 E4
Kilglass, Co Galway	21 C1	Killeevan	9 A7
Kilglass/Cill Ghlais	15 E7	Killeglan	21 D1
Co Roscommon/Ros Comáin		Killeigh/Cill Aichidh	22 J4
Kilglass/Cill Ghlas	6 J6	Killen/Cillín	8 H1
Co Sligo/Sligeach		Killenagh	30 J3
Kilgobnet/Cill Ghobnait	32 G2	Killenaule/Cill Náile	28 K4
Co Kerry/Ciarraí		Co Tipperary/Tiobraid Árann	
Kilgobnet, Co Waterford	35 A2	Killenaule, Co Tipperary	22 F5
Kilgowan	23 D5	Killeshil	22 K2
Kilgrogan	27 B4	Killeter/Coill Íochtair	8 H2
Kilgullane	27 E7	Killimer	26 H3
Kilkea	23 C7	Killimor/Cill Íomair	21 D4
Kilkeasy	29 C5	Killinaboy/Cill Iníne Baoith	20 H6
		Killinardrish/Cill an Ard-doiris	33 C4

Killinaspick	29 C6	Kilmurry, Co Clare	26 H1
Killinchy/Cill Dhuinsí	12 J3	Kilmurry/Cill Mhuire	27 B1
Killincooly	30 J5	Co Clare/An Clár	
Killiney/Cill Iníon Léinin	24 H3	Kilmurry/Cil Mhuire	33 B5
Co Dublin/Baile Átha Cliath		Co Cork Corcaigh	
Killiney, Co Kerry	25 D7	Kilmurry, Co Limerick	27 B6
Killinick/Cill Fhionnóg	30 H7	Kilmurry, Co Limerick	27 E4
Killinierin/Coill an Iarainn	30 J2	Kilmurry, Co Wicklow	23 D7
Killinkere/Cillín Chéir	17 B3	Kilmurvy/Cill Mhuirbhigh	19 D4
Killinny	20 J5	Kilmyshall	30 G3
Killinthomas	23 B3	Kilnacarriga	34 J2
Killiskey	24 H5	Kilnacreagh	27 C2
Killmacahill	34 H5	Kilnagross/Coill na gCros	16 F2
Killmore Upper	16 F5	Kilnahown	21 D3
Killogeary	6 G6	Kilnaleck/Cill na Leice	16 K3
Killogeenaghan	22 G2	Kilnamanagh/Cill na Manach	30 J4
Killaghteen	26 K5	Kilnamona/Cill na Móna	20 H7
Killoluaig	31 C4	Kilntown	10 G4
Killomoran	20 K5	Kilpatrick	33 D6
Killoneen	23 A3	Kilpedder	24 H5
Killoran/Cil Odhráin	21 C3	Kilquane	31 C1
Killorglin/Cill Orglan	32 F2	Kilquiggin	30 G1
Killoscobe	21 B1	Kilraghts/Cill Reachtais	4 F4
Killough/Cill Locha	12 J6	Kilrane/Cill Ruáin	30 J7
Killsallaghan	24 G1	Kilrea/Cill Ria	3 E5
Killucan/Cill Liúcainne	17 A7	Kilrean/Cill Riáin	1 C7
Killukin	15 E3	Kilreekill/Cili Ricill	21 C3
Killurin/Cill Liúráin	30 G6	Kilroghter	20 J2
Killurly	31 C5	Kilronan/Cill Rónáin	19 D5
Killusty	28 K5	Kilross/Cill Ros	28 F5
Killybegs, Co Antrim	4 F7	Kilrush/Cill Rois	26 G3
Killybegs/Na Cealla Beaga	7 C2	Kilsallagh/Coill Salach	15 B6
Co Donegal/Dun na nGall		Co Galway/Gaillimh	
Killyclogher	8 K2	Kilsallagh/Coil Salach	13 D4
Killygar	16 H2	Co Mayo/Maigh Eo	
Killygordon/Cúil na gCuiridin	2 G7	Kilsaran	18 F3
Killykergan/Coill Ui Chiaragain	3 D5	Kilshanchoe	23 C2
Killylea/Coillidh Léith	9 C5	Kilshannig	25 D7
Killyleagh/Cill Ó Laoch	12 J4	Kilshanny/Cill Seanaigh	20 G6
Killyneill/Coill Ui Néill	9 C6	Kilsheeland	28 K6
Killyon	22 G5	Kilshinahan	33 C7
Killyrover	8 J6	Kilskeer/Cill Scíre	17 B5
Kilmacanoge/Cill Mocheanóg	24 H4	Kilskeery/Cill Scíre	8 H4
Kilmacow/Cill Mhic Bhúith	29 C7	Kiltamagh	14 J4
Kilmacrenan/Cill Mhic Réanáin	2 G4	Kiltarsaghaun	14 F5
Kilmacthomas/Coill Mhic Thomáisín	35 B1	Kiltartan	20 K5
Kilmactranny/Cili Mhic Treana	15 D1	Kiltealy/Cill Téile	30 F4
Kilmaganny/Cill Mogeanna	29 B5	Kilteel/Cill Tile	23 E3
Kilmaine/Cill Mheáin	14 H7	Kiltealy/Cill Tíle	27 E4
Kilmainham Wood/		Kiltegan	23 E7
Cill Maighneann	17 C4	Kiltiernan/Cill Tiarnáin	24 H3
Kilmalady	22 H2	Co Dublin/Baile Átha Cliath	
Kilmaley/Cill Mháille	26 K1	Kiltiernan, Co Galway	20 K4
Kilmalin	24 G4	Kiltober	22 J2
Kilmallock/Cill Mocheallóg	27 D6	Kiltoom/Cill Tuama	21 E1
Kilmanagh/Cill Mhanach	29 A3	Co Roscommon/Ros Comáin	
Kilmaniheen	26 H6	Kiltoom, Co Westmeath	16 K6
Kilmeadan/Cill Mhíodháin	29 C7	Kiltormer/Cill Tormóir	21 D3
Kilmeage/Cill Maodhog	23 C3	Kiltullagh/Cill Tulach	21 A3
Kilmeedy/Cill Míde	27 A6	Kiltyclogher/Coilte Clochair	7 E5
Kilmessan/Cill Mheasáin	17 D7	Kilvemnon	29 A5
Kilmichael/Cill Mhichíl	33 A5	Kilvine	14 K6
Kilmihil/Cill Mhichíl	26 J2	Kilwatermoy	34 J2
Kilmona	33 E3	Kilwaughter/Cill Uachtair	4 J6
Kilmoon	35 D6	Kilwoghan	23 E2
Kilmore Quay/		Kilworth/Cill Uird	34 G1
Cé na Cille Móire	36 H1	Kilworth Camp	34 G1
Kilmore/An chill Mhór	9 E4	Kinard	26 J4
Co Armagh/Ard Mhacha		Kinawley/Cill Náile	8 H6
Kilmore, Co Cavan	16 J2	Kingarrow	1 E6
Kilmore/An Chill Mhór	27 D2	Kingscourt/Dún an Rí	17 C3
Co Clare/An Clár		Kingsland	15 C3
Kilmore/An Chill Mhór	10 K4	Kingsmill	9 D2
Co Down		Kingsmills	10 F6
Kilmore, Co Mayo	14 H2	Kinlough/Cionn Locha	7 D4
Kilmore/Cill Mhór	15 E3	Kinnegad/Cionn Átha Gad	23 A1
Co Roscommon/Ros Comáin		Kinnitty/Cionn Eitigh	22 G5
Kilmore/An chill Mhór	36 H1	Kinsale/Cionn tSáile	33 E6
Co Wexford/Loch Garman		Kinsalebeg/Baile an Phoill	34 K3
Kilmorna/Coill Mhaonaigh	26 H5	Kinsaley	24 H1
Kilmorony	23 B7	Kinvarra, Co Galway	19 E2
Kilmovee	15 A3	Kinvarra/Cinn Mhara	20 J4
Kilmuckridge/Cill Mhucraise	30 J4	Co Galway/Gaillimh	
Kilmurrin	35 C2	Kircubbin/Cill Ghobáin	12 J3
Kilmurry McMahon/			
Cill Mhuire Mhic Mhathúna	26 J3		

Kirkhills	3	E4
Kirkistown	12	K4
Kishkeam/Coiscéim na Cailli	33	A1
Knights Town	31	C4
Knock/An Cnoc Co Clare/An Clár	26	H3
Knock/An Cnoc Co Mayo/Maigh Eo	14	J4
Knock/An Cnoc Co Tipperary/Tiobraid Árann	22	H7
Knockacaurhin	20	H7
Knockaderry/Cnoc an Doire	27	A5
Knockagurraun	20	G3
Knockaholet/Cnoc an Chollait	4	F4
Knockainy/Cnoc Áine	27	D5
Knockalaghta	15	C5
Knockalough/Cnoc an Locha	26	J2
Knockalunkard	20	H7
Knockananna/Cnoc an Eanaigh	24	F7
Knockanarra	14	K5
Knockane	33	B5
Knockanevin/Cnocán Aoibhinn	27	E7
Knockanure	26	H5
Knockatian	20	H5
Knockaroe	22	H7
Knockaun	21	C4
Knockaunbrack	26	H6
Knockaunnaglashy	32	F2
Knockaunroe	31	E2
Knockayrogeen	31	C1
Knockboy/An Cnoc Buí	35	A1
Knockbrack, Co Clare	27	D1
Knockbrack/An Cnoc Breac Co Donegal/Dún na nGall	2	H6
Knockbrack, Co Kerry	26	F6
Knockbride	17	B2
Knockbridge/Droichead an Cnoic	17.	E2
Knockbrit/Cnoc an Bhriotaigh	28	J5
Knockbrown	33	C6
Knockburden	33	D5
Knockcloghrim/Cnoc Clochdhroma	3	D7
Knockcroghery/Croc an Chrochaire	15	E7
Knockdarnan	27	C5
Knockdrislagh	33	D2
Knockeenadallane	32	K1
Knockeencreen	26	H7
Knocklofty	28	J6
Knockling/Cnoc Loinge	27	E5
Knockmael	20	K6
Knockmajor	29	C2
Knockmore/An Cnoc Mór	14	H2
Knockmourne	34	H2
Knocknaboley	26	J1
Knocknacurra	33	D6
Knocknagashel/Cnoc na gCais	26	H6
Knocknageeha	14	G7
Knocknagree	32	K2
Knocknahaha	26	F7
Knocknahila	26	H1
Knocknahilan	33	D5
Knocknalina	5	C6
Knocknalower	5	D6
Knocknaskagh	34	H4
Knockraha/Cnoc Rátha	34	F4
Knockroe, Co Cork	35	D5
Knockroe, Co Kerry	31	E4
Knockroe, Co Waterford	35	A2
Knocks, Co Cork	33	B7
Knocks, Co Laois	22	J5
Knockskagh	33	B7
Knockskavane	27	A4
Knocktopher/Cnoc an Tóchair	29	C5
Knuttery	33	E2
Kyle	23	A6
Kyleballyhue	29	E1
Kylebrack/An Choill Bhreac	21	B4
Kylegarve	28	F3

L

Labasheeda/Leaba Shioda	26	J3
Labby	3	C7
Lack/An Leac	8	H3
Lackagh	23	B4
Lackamore/An Leac Mhór	27	E1
Lackan Cross	15	D7
Lackan, Co Carlow	29	D2
Lackan, Co Westmeath	16	J6
Lackan/An Leacain Co Wicklow/Cill Mhantáin	24	F4
Lackareagh	33	B5
Lackbrooder	26	H7
Lacken/Leacain	21	E6
Lackendarragh North	34	F2
Lackey	22	H6
Ladysbridge/ Droichead na Scuab	34	H4
Lagavara	4	F2
Lagganstown	28	H5
Laghey Corner	9	D3
Laghy/An Lathaigh	7	E2
Lahardaun	14	G2
Lakyle	26	J3
Lambeg/Lann Bheag	10	H3
Lamoge	29	B5
Lanesborough/Béal Átha Liag	16	F6
Lannaght	21	A6
Laracor	17	D7
Laragh, Co Kildare	23	D2
Laragh, Co Wicklow	24	G6
Largan, Co Mayo	5	E7
Largan, Co Roscommon	15	E4
Largan, Co Sligo	14	J1
Largy	7	B2
Larne/Latharna	4	K6
Lattin/Laitean	28	F5
Laurelvale/Tamhnaigh Bhealtaine	10	F5
Laurencetown/An Baile Mór	21	D3
Lavagh/Leamhach	15	A1
Lawrencetown/Baile Labhráis	10	F5
Laytown/An Inse	18	G5
Leamlara/Léim Lára	34	G3
Leap/An Léim	36	F5
Lecarrow/An Leithcheathrú	15	E7
Leckemy/Leic Éime	3	A2
Leenaun/An Lionán	13	D6
Legan or Lenamore	16	H6
Leggah	16	H3
Legoniel/Lag an Aoil	10	H2
Lehinch/An Leacht	20	F7
Leighlinbridge/ Leithghlinn an Droichid	29	E2
Leitrim East	26	H4
Leitrim, Co Clare	26	H2
Leitrim/Liatroim Co Leitrim/Liatroim	15	E2
Lemanaghan	22	G3
Lemybrien/Léim Ui Bhriain	35	B1
Leperstown	35	E1
Lerrig	25	E6
Letterbreen/Leitir Bhruin	8	G5
Letterkelly	26	J1
Letterkenny/Leitir Ceanainn	2	G5
Letterloan	3	D4
Lettermacaward/ Leitir Mhic an Bhaird	1	C6
Lettermore	19	D3
Levally/An Leathbhaile Co Galway/Gaillimh	15	A7
Levally, Co Mayo	14	H6
Licketstown	29	C7
Lifford	2	J7
Limavady/Léim an Mhadaidh	3	B4
Limerick/Luimneach	27	C3
Limerick Junction/Gabhal Luimnigh	28	F5
Lisbellaw/Lios Béal Átha	8	J5
Lisburn/Lois na gCearrbhach	10	H3
Liscananaun	20	J2
Liscannor/Lios Ceannúir	20	F7
Liscarney/Lios Cearnaigh	13	E5
Liscarroll/Lios Cearúill	27	B7
Liscasey/Lios Uí Chathasaigh	26	K2
Liscloon/Lios Claon	2	K6
Liscrona	26	F3
Lisdargan	31	D1
Lisdoart/Lios Dubhairt	9	B4
Lisdoonvarna/Lios Dúin Bhearna	20	G6
Lisdowney	29	B1
Lisduff/An Lios Dubh Co Cavan/An Cabhán	17	B4
Lisduff, Co Cork	33	E3

Lisduff, Co Offaly	22	G4
Lisgarode	21	E7
Lisgoold	34	G3
Lisheen	27	A2
Lisheenaguile	21	D4
Liskeagh	15	C2
Lislea/Lios Liath	10	F7
Lismore/Lios Mór	34	J2
Lismoyle	15	E7
Lisnacaffry	16	J5
Lisnacree/Lios na Cri	18	H1
Lisnadill/Lios na Daille	9	D6
Lisnageer/Lios na gCaor	17	A1
Lisnagry/Lios na Grai	27	D3
Lisnakill Cross	35	D1
Lisnamuck/Lios na Muc	3	D7
Lisnarrick/Lios na nDaróg	8	G4
Lisnaskea/Lios na Scéithe	8	J6
Lispatrick	33	E7
Lispole/Lios Póil	31	D1
Lisroe	26	K1
Lisronagh/Lios Ruanach	28	K6
Lisryan	16	J5
Lissaha	28	J4
Lissalway/Lios Sealbhaigh	15	C5
Lissanacody	21	D4
Lissananny	15	B4
Lissarnona	35	C6
Lisselton/Lios Eiltin	26	G5
Lissycasey/Lios Uí Chathasaigh	26	K2
Listellick	26	F7
Listerlin	29	D6
Listoke/Lios Tuathail	26	G5
Lisvarrinane/Lios Fearnáin	28	F6
Littleton/An Baile Beag	28	J3
Lixnaw/Leic Snámha	26	F6
Loanends/Carn Mhéabha	10	H1
Lobinstown/Baile Lóibín	17	D4
Loch Gowna	16	J3
Loghill/Leamhchoill Co Limerick/Liatroim	26	J4
Loghill, Co Limerick	27	A5
Logleagh	34	H1
Lombardstown/Baile Limbaird	33	C2
Londonderry/Doire	2	K5
Longford/An Longfort Co Longford/An Longfort	16	G5
Longford, Co Offaly	22	G5
Longwood/Maigh Dearmahai	23	C1
Lorrha/Lothra	21	E5
Lorum	29	E3
Loskeran	35	A3
Loughaclerybeg	21	B2
Loughacutteen	28	H6
Loughanaboll	6	K7
Loughanavally	22	J1
Loughanleagh	17	C3
Loughbrickland/Loch Bricleann	10	G5
Lougher	31	E1
Loughgall/Loch gCál	9	E4
Loughglinn/Loch Glinne	15	B4
Loughguile/Loch gCaol	4	F4
Loughinisland/Loch an Oileánn	10	K5
Loughmoe/Luachma	28	J2
Loughmorne/Loch Morn	17	C1
Loughrea/Baile Loch Riach	21	B4
Loughshinny	18	H7
Louisburgh/Cluain Cearbán	13	D4
Louth/Lú	17	E2
Lowertown	35	B5
Lowtown	10	H5
Lucan/Leamhcán	24	F2
Lugdoon	6	K6
Luggacurren/Log an Churraigh	23	A7
Lukeswell	29	C6
Lullymore	23	C3
Lurgan/An Lorgain Co Armagh/Ard Mhacha	10	F4
Lurgan, Co Offaly	22	G2
Lurgan/An Lorgain Co Roscommon/Ros Comáin	15	C3
Lurganboy, Co Donegal	2	H3
Lurganboy, Co Leitrim	7	D5
Lusk/Lusca	18	H7
Lyracrumpane/ Ladhar an Chrompáin	26	G6

Lyradane	33	D3
Lyre/ Ladhar an Chrompáin or An Ladhar Co Cork/Corcaigh	33	C2
Lyre, Co Kerry	26	H7
Lyre, Co Waterford	34	H3
Lyrenaglogh	34	H1

M

Maam Cross	19	E1
Maas	1	C7
Mace	14	F4
Mackan/Macan	8	H6
Macosquin/Maigh Choscáin	3	D4
Macroney	34	G1
Macroom/Maigh Chromtha	33	B4
Maddockstown/Baile Mhadóg	29	C3
Maganey/Maigh Geine	23	C7
Maghaberry	10	G3
Maghera Cross	20	K7
Maghera Co Down	10	J6
Maghera/Machaire Rátha Co Londonderry/Doire	3	D6
Magherafelt/Machaire Fíolta	3	D7
Magheralin/Machaire Lainne	10	G4
Magheramason	2	K5
Magheramorne/Machaire Morna	4	K7
Magheraveely/Machaire Mhilie	8	K7
Maghery/An Machaire	1	C6
Magilligan/Aird Mhic Giollagain	3	B3
Maguiresbridge/Droichead Mhig Uidir	8	J6
Mainham	23	D2
Malahide/Mullach Íde	24	H1
Malin/Málainn	2	K1
Mallaranny/An Mhala Raiothni	13	D3
Mallow/Mala	33	D2
Mallusk/Maigh Bhloisce	10	H1
Manorcunningham/ Mainéar Uí Chuinneagáin	2	H5
Manorhamilton/Cluainin	7	D6
Manseltown	28	J2
Mansfieldtown	18	F3
Mantua/An Mointeach	15	D4
Marble Arch	8	G6
Mardyke	28	K4
Margymonaghan	3	B3
Markethill/Cnoc an Mhargaidh	9	E6
Markhamstown	28	J6
Marlfield	28	J6
Marshalstown/Baile Mharascail	30	G4
Martinstown/Baile Ui Mháirtin	4	G5
Marty	17	C5
Masterstown	28	H5
Matehy	33	D4
Maulatrahane	35	E5
Maulavanig	32	J6
Maulawaddra	35	B5
Maum/An Mám	8	E7
Mauricesmills/Muilte Mhuiris	20	H7
Mayglass	30	H7
Maynooth/Maigh Naud	23	E2
Mayo/Maigh Eo	14	H5
Mayobridge/Droichead Mhaigh Eo	10	G7
Mazetown	10	H3
McGaffins Corner	10	G6
McGregor's Corner	4	G5
McLaughlins Corner	3	E5
Meanus/Méanos	27	C4
Meelick	21	E4
Meelin/An Mhaoilinn	26	K7
Meenaclady	1	D3
Meenbannivane	26	H7
Meenglass	2	H5
Meennaraheeny	26	J7
Meirhill	25	E5
Menlough, Co Galway	20	H3
Menlough/Mionlach Co Galway/Gaillimh	21	B1
Middlequarter	34	K1
Middletown/Coillidh Chanannain	9	C6
Midfield/An Trian Láir	14	J3
Midleton/Mainistir na Corann	34	G4
Milehouse/Teach an Nhile	30	G4
Milemill	23	D5

Milestone/Cloch an Mhile	28	G3
Milford/Áth an Mhuilinn Co Armagh/Ard Mhacha	9	D5
Milford/Áth na Muilte Co Cork/Corcaigh	27	B6
Mill Brook	8	K7
Mill Town/Baile an Mhuilinn	10	G1
Millbrook/Sruthán an Mhuilin	4	J6
Milford/Baile na nGallóglach	2	G4
Millisle/Oileán an Mhuilinn	12	J2
Millstreet/Sráid an Mhuilinn Co Cork/Corcaigh	34	G1
Millstreet, Co Cork	33	A2
Millstreet, Co Waterford	34	K1
Milltown Malbay/Sráid na Cathrach	26	H1
Milltown, Co Armagh	9	E5
Milltown, Co Armagh	9	C6
Milltown/Baile an Mhuilinn Co Cavan/An Cabhán	16	J1
Milltown, Co Donegal	7	D2
Milltown, Co Down	10	G7
Milltown, Co Down	10	G6
Milltown/Baile an Mhuilinn Co Dublin/Baile Átha Cliath	24	F2
Milltown/Baile an Mhuilinn Co Galway/Gaillimh	14	K6
Milltown, Co Galway	15	B7
Milltown, Co Kerry	31	C1
Milltown/Baile an Mhuilinn Co Kerry/Ciarraí	32	G1
Milltown, Co Kildare	23	C4
Milltown, Co Kilkenny	29	C6
Milltown, Co Londonderry	3	C3
Milltown, Co Londonderry	3	D4
Milltown, Co Tyrone	9	A2
Milltown, Co Westmeath	16	J7
Milltownpass/ Bealach Bhaile an Mhuilinn	23	A1
Minane Bridge/ Droichead an Mhionnáin	34	F6
Minerstown/Baile na Mianadóirí	10	K6
Minorstown	29	A6
Minterburn/Muintir Bhirn	9	C4
Mitchelstown/Baile Mhistéale	28	F7
Moanmore, Co Clare	26	G3
Moanmore, Co Tipperary	27	E5
Moate/An Móta	22	G2
Modelligo	34	K2
Modrenny	21	E7
Mogeely/Maigh Dhíle	34	H4
Mohil	29	C2
Mohill/Maothail	16	F3
Moira/Maigh Rath	10	G3
Monaghan/Muineachán	9	B6
Monagoun	34	H2
Monaincha Bog	22	G7
Monalour	34	J1
Monamolin/Muine Moling	30	J4
Monamraher	35	A3
Monaseed/Móin na Saighead	30	H2
Monaster/An Mhainistir	27	C4
Monasteraden/Mainistir Réadáin	15	B3
Monasterevin/Mainistir Eimhin	23	B4
Monea/Maigh Niadh	8	G5
Moneen, Co Clare	25	E4
Moneen, Co Galway	20	J1
Monettia Beg	22	J4
Moneycusker	33	A5
Moneydig/Muine Dige	3	D5
Moneygall/Muine Gall	22	F7
Moneyglass/An Muine Glas	4	F7
Moneymore/Muine Mór	9	D1
Moneyneany/Món na nIonadh	3	C7
Moneyreagh/Monadh Riabhach	10	K3
Monilea/An Muine Liath	16	K7
Monivea/Muine Mhéa	21	A2
Monkstown/Baile na Manach Co Antrim/Aontroim	10	J1
Monkstown/Baile na Mhanach Co Cork/Corcaigh	34	F5
Montpelier	27	D2
Mooncoin/Móin Choinn	29	C7
Moone/Maoin	23	C6
Moord	34	K4
Moorfields/Páirc an tSléibhe	4	G7
Morenane	27	B5
Mornington/Baile Uí Mhornáin	18	G5
Moroe/Maigh Rua	27	E3
Mortlestown	27	D6
Moskeagh	33	C5
Mosney Camp	18	G6
Moss-side/Mas Saíde	4	F3
Mossley/Maslaí	10	J1
Mothel	29	A7
Mount Bellew/An Creagán	21	B1
Mount Nugent/ Droichead Uí Dhálaigh	16	K4
Mount Stewart	12	J3
Mount Talbot/Mun Talbóid	15	D7
Mount Temple/An Grianan	22	G1
Mount Uniacke/Cúil O gCorra	34	H3
Mountallen	15	E1
Mountbolus/Cnocán Bhólais	22	H4
Mountcatherine	34	F3
Mountcharles/Moin Searlas	7	D2
Mountcollins/Cnoc Uí Choileáin	26	J7
Mountfield/Achadh Ard	9	A2
Mountjoy/Muinseo	8	K2
Mountmellick/Móinteach Milie	22	K5
Mountnorris/Achadh na Cranncha	9	E6
Mountrath/Maiglean Rátha	22	J6
Mountshannon/Baile Uí Bhealáin	21	C7
Moveen	26	F3
Moville/Bun an Phobail	3	B3
Moy Co Galway	20	J5
Moy/An Maigh Co Tyrone/Tír Eoghain	9	D4
Moyard/Maigh Ard	13	B7
Moyasta/Maigh Sheasta	26	G3
Moycarky	28	J3
Moycullen/Maigh Cuilinn	20	G2
Moydow/Maigh Dumha	16	G6
Moygashel/Maigh gCaisil	9	D3
Moyglass/Maigh Ghlas	28	J4
Moyle	29	E1
Moylough/Maigh Locha Co Galway/Gaillimh	21	B1
Moylough, Co Sligo	15	A2
Moymore	27	B1
Moynalty/Maigh Locha	17	C4
Moynalvy	23	D1
Moyne	24	F7
Moyne/An Mhaighean Co Roscommom/Ros Comáin	15	B4
Moyne/An Mhaighean Co Tipperary/Tiobraid Árann	28	J2
Moyrahan	5	C6
Moyreen	26	K4
Moyrus	19	C2
Moys	3	B5
Moyvally/Maigh Bhealaigh	23	C1
Moyvore/Maigh Mhórdha	16	H7
Moyvoughly/Maigh Bhachla	22	G1
Mt. Melleray Monastery	34	J1
Muckamore/Maigh Chomair	10	G1
Mucklon	23	C2
Muckrush	20	H2
Muff/Magh	2	K4
Muinganear	26	H7
Muingaphuca	32	F2
Muingwee	26	H6
Muingydowda	31	C4
Mulhuddart/Mullach Eadrad	24	F1
Mullafarry	6	H7
Mullagh/An Mullach Co Cavan/An Cabhán	17	B4
Mullagh/Mullach Co Clare/An Clár	26	H1
Mullagh, Co Galway	21	C4
Mullagh, Co Mayo	13	D5
Mullagh, Co Meath	23	E1
Mullaghbane	17	E1
Mullaghmacormick	16	F4
Mullaghmore/An Mullach Mór	7	C5
Mullaghroe	15	B2
Mullan Head	3	E5
Mullan, Co Londonderry	3	D4
Mullan/An Muileann Co Monaghan/Muineachán	9	C5
Mullany's Cross	14	K1
Mullartown	10	J7
Mullen	15	C4
Mullenaboree	33	E2
Mullennaglogh	29	A5
Mullennakill	29	D5
Mullinacuff/Muileann Mic Dhuibh	30	G1
Mullinahone/Muileann na hUamhan	29	A4
Mullinavat/Muileann an Bhata	29	C6
Mullingar/An Muileann gCear	16	K7
Multyfarnham/Muilte Farannáin	16	K6
Mungret/Mungairit	27	C3
Murher	26	H5
Murntown/Baile Mhúráin	30	H7
Murreagh	31	B1
Murrisk/Muraisc	13	E4
Murroogh	20	G5
Mweennalaa	26	G7
Myross	36	F5
Myshall/Miseal	30	F2

N

Naas/An Nás	23	D4
Nad	33	C2
Nahana	23	A4
Naran	1	C7
Narraghmore/An Fhorrach Mhór	23	C5
Naul/An Aill	18	G6
Navan/An Uaimh	17	D6
Neale/An Éill	14	G7
Nealstown	22	H6
Nedanone	31	E5
Nenagh/An tAonach	28	F1
New Birmingham/Gleann an Ghuail	28	K3
New Buildings/An Baile Nua	2	K5
New Chapel Cross	31	D5
New Inn/An Dromainn Co Cavan/An Cabhán	17	A3
New Inn/An Cnoc Breac Co Galway/Gaillimh	21	B3
New Inn, Co Laois	23	A5
New Kildimo	27	B3
New Ross/Ros Mhic Thriúin	29	E6
New Twopothouse Village/ Tigh Nua an Dá Phota	33	B1
Newbawn/An Bábhún Nua	30	F6
Newbliss/Cúil Darach	9	A7
Newbridge/An Droichead Nua Co Galway/Gaillimh	15	C7
Newbridge, Co Limerick	27	A4
Newcastle West/ An Caisléan Nua	26	K5
Newcastle/An Caisléan Nua Co Down/An Dún	10	J6
Newcastle/An Caisléan Nua Co Dublin/Baile Átha Cliath	23	E3
Newcastle/An Caisléan Nua Co Galway/Gaillimh	21	A2
Newcastle/An Caisléan Nua Co Tipperary/Tiobraid Árann	28	J7
Newcastle/An Caisléan Nua Co Wicklow/Cill Mhantáin	24	H5
Newcestown/Baile Níos	33	C6
Newchapel	28	J6
Newferry	3	E7
Newinn/Loch Ceann	28	H5
Newmarket/Áth Trasna Co Cork/Corcaigh	33	B1
Newmarket, Co Kilkenny	29	C5
Newmarket-on-Fergus/ Cora Chaitlin	27	B2
Newmills, Co Cork	36	G5
Newmills/An Muileann Úr Co Donegal/Dún na nGall	2	G6
Newmills/An Muileann Nua Co Tyrone/Tír Eoghain	9	D3
Newport/Baile Uí Fhiacháin Co Mayo/Maigh Eo	13	E3
Newport/An Port Nua Co Tipperary/Tiobraid Árann	27	E2
Newry/An tIur	10	F7
Newtown Bellew	21	B1
Newtown Cashel/ Baile Nua an Chaisil	16	F7
Newtown Cloghans/An Baile Ur	14	H1
Newtown Cunningham/An Baile Nua	2	J5
Newtown Forbes/An Lois Breac	16	G5
Newtown, Co Galway	21	B3
Newtown, Co Kildare	23	D2
Newtown, Co Kilkenny	29	A3
Newtown, Co Laois	29	D1
Newtown, Co Limerick	27	D5
Newtown, Co Mayo	14	G4
Newtown, Co Meath	17	E4
Newtown, Co Offaly	21	E4
Newtown, Co Roscommon	21	D2
Newtown, Co Roscommon	15	C5
Newtown, Co Tipperary	28	F5
Newtown, Co Tipperary	22	G7
Newtown, Co Waterford	35	A2
Newtown, Co Waterford	34	K3
Newtown, Co Wexford	36	H1
Newtown, Co Wexford	36	G1
Newtown Gore/An Dúcharraig	16	H1
Newtown-Crommelin/ Baile Nua Chromlain	4	G5
Newtown-Sandes/Maigh Mheain	26	H5
Newtownabbey/ Baile na Mainstreach	10	J1
Newtownadam	28	H6
Newtownards/Baile Nua na hArda	12	H2
Newtownbutler/An Baile Nua	8	K7
Newtownhamilton/Baile Úr	9	E7
Newtownlow	22	J2
Newtownlynch	20	J4
Newtownmountkennedy/ Baile an Chinnéidigh	24	H5
Newtownshandrum/ Baile Nua Sheandroma	27	B6
Newtownstewart/An Baile Nua	8	K1
Nicholastown	29	D7
Ninemilehouse/ Tigh na Naoi Mile	29	A5
Nobber/An Obair	17	D4
Nohaval/Nuach a Bháil	34	F6
North Ring	33	C7
Nórthlands/ An Táchairt Thuaidh	17	C2
Noughaval, Co Clare	20	H6
Noughaval, Co Clare	27	A1
Nurney/An Urnai Co Carlow/Ceatharlach	29	E2
Nurney/An Urnai Co Kildare/Cill Dara	23	C5
Nutts Corner/Coirnéal Nutt	10	G2

O

Oaghley	26	G5
Oatfield	27	C2
Oghill	21	D3
Ogonnelloe/Tuath ÓgConáile	21	B7
Oilgate/Maolán na nGabhar	30	G5
Old Head	33	E7
Old Kilcullen	23	D5
Old Kildimo	27	B3
Old Ross	29	E6
Old Town, Co Laois	22	K7
Old Town/An Seanbhaile Co Roscommon/Ros Comair	21	E3
Old Town, Co Wexford	30	F4
Oldcastle/An Seanchaisleán	17	A4
Oldgrange	28	J7
Oldleigh	23	B7
Oldleighlin/Seanleithghlinn	29	D2
Oldtown, Co Dublin	18	G7
Oldtown, Co Roscommon	22	F2
Omagh/An Ómaigh	8	K2
Omeath/Ó Meith	18	G1
Onaght	19	D4
Oola/Úlla	28	F4
Oranmore/Órán Mór	20	J3
Oristown	17	C5
Oritor/Na Coracha Beaga	9	C2
Oughtdarra	20	G5
Oughter	22	H3
Oughterard/Uachtar Ard	20	G1
Oulart/An tAbhallort	30	H4
Outeragh	28	H6
Ovens/Na hUamhanna	33	D4

Owenbeg/An Abhainn Bheag 6 J6
Owenbristy 20 K4
Owning/Ónainn 29 B6

P

Palace/An Phailis 30 F5
Palatine 29 E1
Palatine Street 27 E4
Pallas Green/An tSeanphailis 27 E4
Pallas Green (new)/Pailis Ghréine 27 E4
Pallas, Co Galway 21 C2
Pallas, Co Laois 22 K6
Pallasboy 22 K2
Pallaskenry/
Droichead an Mhionnáin 34 B3
Pallis 30 J2
Palmerstown/Baile Phámar 24 F2
Park 36 H1
Parkacunna 34 F1
Parkbane 33 C6
Parkgate 10 H1
Parkmore/An Phairc Mhór 20 J4
Parteen 27 C2
Partry/Partraí 14 G5
Passage West/An Pasáiste 34 F5
Passage, Co Roscommon 15 C7
Passage, Co Waterford 29 D7
Patrickswell/Tobar Phádraig 27 C3
Peak 21 B3
Peterswell/Tobar Pheadair 21 A5
Pettigoe/Paiteagó 8 J3
Pharis/Fáras 4 F4
Piercetown, Co Cork 33 E4
Piercetown, Co Wexford 30 H7
Pike 21 E5
Pike Corner 17 D7
Pike of Rush Hall/An Paidhc 22 J7
Piltown/Baile an Phoill 29 B6
Pluck 2 H5
Plumbridge/Droichead an Phlum 2 K7
Pollagh, Co Galway 20 J4
Pollagh/Pollach 22 G3
Co Offaly/Uíbh Fhailí
Pollatlugga 21 C3
Pollboy 21 D3
Pollshask 15 B6
Pomeroy/Pomeroy 9 B2
Pontoon 14 H2
Port 18 G4
Port Laoise/Port Laoise 22 K6
Portacloy 5 D5
Portadown/Port an Dúnáin 10 F4
Portaferry/Port an Pheire 12 J4
Portaleen 3 A1
Portarlington/
Cúil an tSúdaire 23 A4
Portavogie/Port an Bhogaigh 12 K4
Portballintrae/
Port Bhaile an Trá 3 E2
Portglenone/
Port Ghluain Eoghain 3 E6
Portland 21 D5
Portlaw/Port Lách 29 B7
Portmagee/An Caladh 31 B4
Portmarnock/Port Mearnóg 24 H1
Portmuck 4 K6
Portnablagh/Port na Bláiche 2 F3
Portnashangan 16 K6
Portnoo/Port Nua 1 B7
Portraine 18 H7
Portroe/An Port Rua 21 C7
Portrush/Port Rois 3 D2
Portsalon/Port an tSalainn 2 H1
Portstewart/Port Stiobhaird 3 D3
Portumna/Port Omna 21 D5
Pottore 16 F1
Poulnamucky 28 J6
Power's Cross/Crois an Phaoraigh 21 C5
Poyntz Pass/Pas an Phointe 10 F6
Priest Town 34 K1
Priestnaggard 29 E7
Prosperous/An Chorrchoill 23 D3
Puckaun/Pocán 21 D7

Q

Quarrytown 4 G6
Querrin/An Cuibhreann 26 G3
Quilty/Coilte 26 H1
Quin/Cuinche 27 B1

R

Radestown 29 C2
Raffrey/Rafraidh 10 K4
Rahan/Raithean 22 H3
Raharney/Rath Fhearna 17 B7
Raheen, Co Carlow 30 G1
Raheen, Co Cork 33 D5
Raheen, Co Kerry 32 J2
Raheen, Co Kilkenny 29 B6
Raheen, Co Tipperary 28 H6
Raheen, Co Westmeath 22 H1
Raheen/An Ráithin 30 F6
Co Wexford/Loch Garman
Raheenlusk 30 J4
Rake Street 14 G1
Ramsgrange/An Ghráinseach 29 E7
Ranamackan 21 C4
Randalstown/Baile Raghnaill 4 F7
Rapemills 22 F5
Raphoe/Ráth Bhoth 2 H6
Rascalstreet 33 A1
Rasharkin/Ros Earcáin 3 E5
Rashedoge 2 G5
Rath 22 G5
Rath Luire (Charleville) 27 C6
Rathangan/Rath Iomgháin 23 B4
Rathanny 26 G7
Rathaspick 16 H6
Rathbrit 28 J5
Rathcabban/Ráth Cabáin 21 E5
Rathconor 15 D5
Rathconrath/Ráth Conarta 16 J7
Rathcoole 24 F3
Rathcore/Rath Cuair 23 C1
Rathcormack/Ráth Chormaic 34 G2
Rathcrony 26 K1
Rathdangan/Ráth Daingin 23 E7
Rathdowney/Rath Domhnaigh 28 K1
Rathdrum/Ráth Droma 24 G7
Rathduff 16 H6
Ratheenroe 35 C5
Rathernan 23 C3
Rathfeigh/Ráth Faiche 18 F6
Rathfilode 34 F3
Rathfriland/Ráth Fraoileann 10 H6
Rathfylane 30 F5
Rathgarry 29 C1
Rathgormuck/Ráth Ó gCormaic 29 A7
Rathgranagher 14 H6
Rathkeale/Ráth Caola 27 A4
Rathkeevin 28 J6
Rathkenny/Ráth Cheannaigh 17 D5
Rathkeva 15 C4
Rathkineely 15 C4
Rathlackan 6 G6
Rathlee/Ráth Lao 6 J6
Rathlyon 30 F1
Rathmaiden 35 B1
Rathmelton/Ráth Mealtain 2 H4
Rathmore/An Rath Mhór 32 K2
Co Kerry/Ciarraí
Rathmore/An Ráth Mhór 23 E4
Co Kildare/Cill Dara
Rathmoylan 35 E2
Rathmoylon 23 C1
Rathmullan/Ráth Maoláin 2 H4
Rathnew/Ráth Naoi 24 H6
Rathnure/Ráth an Iúir 30 F5
Rathoma 6 G7
Rathorgan 34 H3
Rathowen 16 J6
Rathroeen 6 H7
Rathruane 35 C5
Rathvilly/Ráth Bhile 23 D7
Rathwire 17 A7
Ratoath/Ráth Tó 18 F7
Ratoonagh 35 B5

Ravensdale/
Gleann na BhFiach 18 G1
Ravernet/Rath Bhearnait 10 H3
Ray/An Ráith 2 H4
Reaghstown 17 E3
Reanaclogheen 35 A3
Reanascreena/Rae na Scríne 33 A7
Rear Cross/Crois na Rae 28 F3
Recess/Sraith salach 19 D1
Reclain 9 C3
Redcross/Chrois Dhearg, An 24 H7
Redgate 30 H5
Redhills/An Croc Rua 16 K1
Redwood 21 E5
Rerrin/Raerainn 32 F7
Revallagh 3 E3
Rhode/Ród 23 A2
Richill/Log an Choire 9 E5
Riesk 34 G3
Ring/An Rinn 36 K1
Ringaskiddy/Rinn an Seidigh 34 F5
Ringsend/Droichead an Carraige 3 D4
Ringstown 22 J6
Ringville/An Rinn 35 A3
Rinneen, Co Clare 20 F7
Rinneen, Co Cork 35 E5
Rinville 20 J3
Riverchapel 30 J3
Riverstick/Áth an Mhaide 33 E6
Riverstown, Co Cork 34 F4
Riverstown/Baile Idir dhá 7 C7
Co Sligo/Sligeach
Riverstown/Baile Uí Lachnáin 22 F5
Co Tipperary/Tiobraid Árann
Roadford 20 F6
Robertstown/Baile Ríobaird 23 C3
Robinstown/Baile Ríobín 17 D6
Co Meath/An Mhí
Robinstown, Co Wexford 30 G7
Rochestown, Co Kilkenny 29 C6
Rochestown, Co Kilkenny 29 D7
Rochestown, Co Tipperary 28 H7
Rochfortbridge/
Droichead Chaisleán Loiste 22 K1
Rockchapel/Séipéal na Carraige 26 K7
Rockcorry/Búiochar 17 B1
Rockhill 27 C5
Rockmills 34 F1
Rockstown 24 H7
Rodeen 15 E3
Roevehagh 20 K4
Rooaun 21 E4
Roonah Quay 13 C4
Roosky, Co Mayo 15 A2
Roosky/Rúscaigh 16 F4
Co Roscommon/Ros Comáin
Rooty Cross 21 E2
Rosapenna 2 G3
Rosbercon 29 D6
Roscat 30 F1
Roscommon/Ros Comáin 15 D6
Roscrea/Ros Cré 22 G7
Rosegreen/Faiche Ró 28 J5
Rosenallis/
Ros Fhionnghlaise 22 J5
Rosmuck/Ros Muc 19 E2
Rosmult 28 H3
Rosnakill/Ros na Cille 2 G3
Ross Behy 31 E2
Ross Port/Ros Dumhach 5 D6
Ross, Co Cork 36 F5
Ross/An Ros 16 K4
Co Meath/An Mhí
Rossadrehid/Ros an Droichead 28 G6
Rossanean 32 H1
Rossaveal 19 E3
Rossbrin 35 C5
Rosscahill/Ros Cathail 20 G2
Rosses Point/An Ros 7 B5
Rossinver/Ros Inbhir 7 E5
Rosslare/Ros Láir 30 J7
Rosslea/Ros Liath 9 A6
Rossmore, Co Cork 33 A5
Rossmore/An Ros Mór 33 B7
Co Cork/Corcaigh
Rossmore, Co Laois 29 D1

Rossmore, Co Monaghan 9 B6
Rossnowlagh/Ros Neamhlach 7 D3
Rostellan/Ros Tialláin 34 G5
Rostrevor/Ros Treabhair 18 G1
Rosturk 13 D3
Roundfort 14 H6
Roundstone/Cloch na Rón 19 C1
Rousky 9 A1
Ruan/An Ruán 20 J7
Rubane/Rú Bán 12 K3
Rush/An Ros 18 H7
Rusheeny 20 F1
Russellstown 28 J7
Ryehill 21 A2
Rylane Cross 33 C3

S

Saggart/Teach Sagard 24 F3
Saint Johnstown 2 J6
Saintfield/Tamhnaigh Naomh 10 K4
Sallahig 31 D4
Sallins/Na Solláin 23 B3
Sallybrook 34 F4
Sallypark 28 G1
Saltmills/Muileann an tSáile 36 F1
Sandholes/Glais an Ghainimh 9 C2
Sandyford/Áth an Ghainimh 24 G3
Santry/Seantrabh 24 G1
Saul 12 J5
Scardaun, Co Mayo 14 J6
Scardaun, Co Roscommon 15 D7
Scarriff/An Scairbh 21 B7
Scartaglin 32 J1
Scarva/Scarbhach 10 F5
Scotch Corner 9 C7
Scotch Street/
Sráid na hAlbanach 9 E4
Scotshouse/Teach an Scotaigh 16 K1
Scotstown/Baile an Scotaigh 9 B6
Scrahan 25 E7
Scrahanfadda 32 K2
Scramoge/Scramóg 15 E5
Scrarour 34 F1
Screen/An Scrín 30 H7
Screggan/An Screagán 22 H3
Scriggan 3 B5
Scurlockstown 17 C5
Seaforde/Baile Forda 10 K5
Seapatrick 10 G5
Seskin 28 K6
Seskinore/Seisceann Odhar 8 K3
Sess Kilgreen/
Seisíoch Chill Ghrianna 9 B4
Shanagarry/An Seangharraí 34 H5
Shanaglish 20 K6
Shanagolden/Seanghualainn 26 K4
Shanahoe/Seanchua 22 J7
Shanballard 21 B2
Shanbally/An Seanbhaile 34 F5
Co Cork/Corcaigh
Shanbally, Co Galway 15 B7
Shanbally, Co Waterford 35 B2
Shanballyedmond 28 F3
Shanballymore/An Seanbhaile Mór 33 E1
Shaneacrane 32 K6
Shangarry 21 C4
Shankill/Seanchill 24 H3
Shanlaragh/Seanlárach 33 A6
Shannakea/Seanachae 26 K3
Shannon Harbour/
Caladh na Sionainne 22 F4
Shannonbridge/
Droichead na Sionainne 21 E3
Shannonville 21 C7
Shanragh 23 B7
Shanrahan 28 G2
Shanrath 27 A6
Shantonagh/Seantonnach 17 C1
Shanvogh 26 J1
Sharavogue/Searbhóg 22 F6
Shercock/Searcóg 17 C1
Sheskin 5 E7
Shevry 28 C2
Shillelagh/Síol Ealaigh 30 G2
Shinrone/Suían Róin 22 F6
Shrigley 12 J4

Place	Map	Grid
Shrone	26	G4
Shronell	28	F5
Shronowen/Srón Abhann	26	G4
Shrule/Sruthair	14	H7
Sillahertane	32	K6
Silver Bridge/Béal Átha an Airgid	17	E1
Silver Stream	9	B6
Silvermines/Béal Átha Gabhann	28	F1
Sion Mills/Muileann an tSiáin	2	J7
Six Crosses	26	G5
Six Road End	12	J2
Sixmilebridge/Droichead Abhann	27	B2
Sixmilecross/Na Coracha Móra	9	A3
Skahanagh	32	J6
Skahanagh North	34	F3
Skahanagh South	34	F3
Skeagh, Co Cork	35	D5
Skeagh, Co Westmeath	16	H7
Skehanagh, Co Galway	20	K5
Skehanagh, Co Galway	21	A1
Skeheen	28	F7
Skerries/Na Sceiri	18	H6
Skibbereen/An Sciobairín	35	E5
Skreen, Co Meath	17	E6
Skreen/An Scrin Co Sligo/Sligeach	7	A6
Skull/An Scoil	35	C5
Slane/Baile Shláine	17	E5
Slieveroe/Sliabh Rua	29	D7
Sligo/Sligeach	7	B6
Smithborough/Na Mullai	9	A6
Smithstown	29	C1
Sneem/An tSnaidhm	31	E5
Spa/An Spá	25	E7
Spanish Point/Rinn na Spáinneach	26	H1
Sperrin	3	B7
Spiddle	20	G3
Spink	23	A7
Spittaltown	22	H2
Spring Town	2	K5
Springfield/Achadh an Fhuaráin	8	G5
Sraghmore	24	G5
Srah	5	C7
Srahanboy	22	H6
Sraheens/Na Sraithíní	13	C3
Srahmore/An Srath Mór	5	D7
Sruh	34	J1
St Margaret's	24	G1
Stabannan	18	F3
Stackallan/Stigh Colláin	17	E5
Staffordstown/Baile Stafard	10	F1
Stamullin	18	G6
Staplestown	23	D2
Steen's Corner	4	G7
Stepaside	24	G3
Stewartstown/An Chraobh	9	D2
Stickstown	33	C5
Stillorgan	24	H3
Stone Bridge	9	A7
Stonepark	27	D4
Stonyford, Co Antrim	10	H2
Stonyford/Áth Stúin Co Kilkenny/Cill Chainnigh	29	C4
Stormont	10	K2
Strabane/An Strath Bán	2	J7
Stradbally	23	A6
Stradbally/An tSraidbhaile	35	B2
Stradone/Sraith an Domhain	17	A2
Straffan/Teach Srafáin	23	E3
Strahart/Sraith Airt	30	G3
Straid/An tSráid	4	J7
Strand/An Trá	26	K6
Strandhill/An Leathros	7	B6
Strangford/Baile Loch Cuan	12	J5
Stranocum/Sraith Nócam	4	F3
Stranorlar/Srath an Urláir	2	G7
Stratford/Áth na Sráiole	23	D6
Streamstown, Co Galway	13	B7
Streamstown/Baile an tSruthain Co Westmeath/An Iarmhi	22	H1
Street/An tSráid	16	J5
Strokestown/Béal na mBuillí	15	E4
Summer Cove	33	E6
Summerhill/Cnoc an Linsigh	23	D1
Suncroft/Crochta na Gréine	23	C5
Swan	23	A7
Swanlinbar/An Muilcann Iarainn	8	G7
Swatragh/An Suaitreach	3	D6
Swinford/Béal Átha na Muice	14	J3
Swords/Sord	24	G1

T

Place	Map	Grid
Taghmon/Teach Munna	30	G7
Taghshinny	16	H6
Tagoat/Teach Gót	30	J7
Tallaght/Tamhlacht	24	F3
Tallanstown/Baile an Tallúnaigh	17	E3
Tallow/Tulach an Iarainn	34	H2
Tallowbridge	34	H2
Tamlaght/Tamhlacht Co Fermanagh/Fear Manach	8	H5
Tamlaght, Co Londonderry	3	E6
Tamnamore/An Tamhnach Mhór	9	D3
Tandragee/Tóin re Gaoith	10	F5
Tang/An Teanga	16	G7
Tankardstown	27	C6
Tara/Teamhair	22	H2
Tarbert/Tairbeart	26	H4
Tarmon/An Tearmann	26	H3
Tassagh/An Tasach	9	D6
Tawny/An Tamhnaigh	2	G3
Tawnyinah	14	K3
Tedagh	32	H7
Tedavnet/Tigh Damhnata	9	B6
Tedd	8	H3
Teemore	8	J7
Teer	25	C7
Teeranearagh	31	C4
Teeravane	31	B1
Teerelton/Tír Eiltín	33	B5
Teermaclane/Tír Mhic Calláin	27	A1
Teevurcher/Taobh Urchair	17	C3
Templeboy/Teampall Baoith	6	K6
Templederry/Teampall Doire	28	G2
Templeetney	28	K6
Templemartin/Teampall Mártan	33	C5
Templemore/An Teampall Mór	28	J1
Templenoe	32	G5
Templeoran	22	K2
Templepark	22	F7
Templepatrick/Teampall Phádraig	10	H1
Templeshanbo/Teampall Seanbhoth	30	F4
Templetouhy/Teampall Tuaithe	28	J1
Templetown	36	F1
Templeusque	34	F4
Tempo/An tIompú Deiseal	8	J5
Termon Rock	9	B2
Termonbarry	16	F5
Termonfeckin/Tearmann Feichín	18	G4
Terryglass/Tír Dha Ghlas	21	D5
Tevrin	17	A7
The Bush	18	G2
The Butts	29	D2
The Cock	10	K4
The Cross/An Chrois	2	K5
The Curragh/An Currach	23	C4
The Diamond/An Diamant Co Antrim/Aontroim	10	G2
The Diamond, Co Tyrone	9	E2
The Downs/Na Dúnta	17	A7
The Drones	4	F4
The Dry Arch	4	F3
The Five Roads	18	G7
The Harrow	30	H4
The Leap	30	F6
The Loup/An Lúb	9	E1
The Pigeons/Na Colúir	16	G7
The Pike, Co Tipperary	21	E6
The Pike, Co Waterford	35	B2
The Pike, Co Waterford	34	J3
The Quarter	3	D5
The Rock/An Charraig	9	C2
The Rower/An Robhar	29	E5
The Sheddings	4	H6
The Spa/An Spá	10	J5
The Sweep	29	B6
The Temple/An Teampall	10	J3
Thomas Street	21	D1
Thomastown/Baile Mhic Andáin Co Kilkenny/Cill Chainnigh	29	C4
Thomastown, Co Limerick	27	E6
Thomastown, Co Meath	17	C4
Thomastown, Co Tipperary	28	G5
Thornton	23	D5
Three Wells	24	G7
Thurles/Durlas	28	J3
Tibohine/Tigh Baoithán	15	B3
Tiduff	25	D5
Tikincor	28	K6
Timahoe, Co Kildare	23	C2
Timahoe/Tigh Mochua Co Laois/Laois	23	A6
Timoleague/Tigh Molaige	33	C7
Timolin	23	C6
Tinahely/Tigh na hÉille	30	H1
Tinmuck	22	G2
Tinnakilla	30	G6
Tipperary/Tiobraid Árann	28	F5
Tirkane/Tír Chiana	3	D6
Tirnaneill	9	B6
Tirneevin	20	K5
Toames/Tuaim	33	B5
Tober, Co Cavan	7	E7
Tober, Co Offaly	22	H2
Toberbeg	23	D6
Tobercurry/Tobar an Choire	15	A1
Toberelatan	21	A4
Tobermore/An Tobar Mór	3	D7
Tobernadarry	14	H7
Toberscanavan	7	B7
Toem/Tuaim	28	F4
Togher or Roundwood	24	G5
Togher, Co Louth	18	G4
Togher, Co Meath	23	C1
Togher, Co Offaly	23	A2
Togher, Co Wicklow	23	E5
Togherbane	25	E6
Tomhaggard/Teach Moshagard	36	J1
Tonabrocky	20	H3
Tonlegee	14	F5
Tonyduff/An Tonnaigh Dhubh	17	B2
Toom/Tuaim	33	A6
Toomaghera	20	G6
Toomard/Tuaim Ard	15	B7
Toombeola	19	C1
Toome/Droichead Thuama	3	E7
Toomyvara/Tuaim Uí Mheára	28	G1
Toor/An Tuar	28	F2
Tooraneena	35	A1
Tooraree	26	J4
Tooreen/An Tuairín	33	E2
Tooreencahill	32	K1
Tooreendermot	26	K7
Toorgarriff	33	E2
Toormakeady/Tuar Mhic Éadaigh	14	F6
Toormore/An Tuar Mór	35	B5
Torque	22	J2
Towergare	35	D1
Tracton	34	F6
Tralee/Trá Lí	26	F7
Tramore/Trá Mhór	35	D1
Trasternagh	21	A1
Trawlebane	32	J7
Trean	14	F6
Treantagh/Na Treantacha	2	G5
Trien/An Trian	15	B5
Trillick/Trileac	8	J4
Trim/Baile Átha Troim	17	D7
Trust	21	C2
Tuam/Tuaim	14	K7
Tuamgraney/Tuaim Gréine	21	B7
Tubber/An Tobar	20	K6
Tubbrid, Co Kilkenny	29	A2
Tubbrid, Co Tipperary	28	H7
Tulla/An Tulach Co Clare/An Clár	20	J5
Tulla, Co Clare	20	K7
Tullagh	32	K5
Tullaghaboy	26	J1
Tullaghan/An Tulachán	7	C4
Tullagher/Tulachar	29	D5
Tullaghought	29	B5
Tullaherin	29	C4
Tullamore, Co Kerry	26	G5
Tullamore/Tulach Mhór Co Offaly/Uíbh Fhailí	22	J3
Tullaree	25	D7
Tullaroan/Tulach Ruáin	29	A3
Tullassa	26	K1
Tullig, Co Clare	25	E3
Tullig, Co Kerry	26	G6
Tullig, Co Kerry	32	F2
Tullow/An Tulach	30	F1
Tullyallen/Tulaigh Álainn	18	F5
Tullycanna	30	G7
Tully Cross	13	C6
Tullyhogue/Tulaigh Óg	9	D2
Tullylease	27	A7
Tullyroan Corner	9	D4
Tullyvin/Tulaigh Bhinn	17	A1
Tulrohaun/Tulach Shrutháin	14	K5
Tulsk/Tuilsce	15	D4
Tuosist/Tuath Ó Siosta	32	F5
Turlough, Co Clare	20	H5
Turlough/Turlach Co Mayo/Maigh Eo	14	H3
Turloughmore/An Turlach Mór	20	K2
Turnaspidogy	32	K5
Turnpike Cross	33	E1
Turreen	16	F6
Twomileborris/Buiríos Léith	28	J3
Tylas	17	E7
Tynagh/Tíne	21	C4
Tynan/Tuineán	9	C5
Tyrella	10	K6
Tyrrellspass/Bealach an Tirialaigh	22	K2

U

Place	Map	Grid
Unionhall/Breéantrá	36	F5
Upperchurch/An Teampall Uachtarach	28	G2
Upperlands/Áth an Phortáin	3	D6
Upton/Garraí Thancaird	33	D6
Urlaur/Urlár	15	A3
Urlingford/Áth na nUrlainn	28	K2

V

Place	Map	Grid
ValleymountAn Chrois	23	E5
Ventry/Ceann Trá	31	B1
Vicarstown/Baile an Bhoicáire	23	B5
Victoria Bridge/Droichead Victoria	2	J7
Villierstown/An Baile Nua	34	K2
Virginia/Achadh an Iuir	17	B4

W

Place	Map	Grid
Walshtown	34	G3
Walterstown	17	E6
Ward/An Barda	24	G1
Waringsford/Áth an Bhairinigh	10	H5
Waringstown/Baile an Bhairinigh	10	G4
Warrenpoint/An Pointe	18	G1
Watch Ho. Village	30	G2
Waterfall/Tobar an Iarla	33	E5
Waterford/Port Láirge	29	D7
Watergrasshill/Cnocán na Biolraí	34	F3
Waterloo	33	D4

Waterville/*An Coireánn*   **31**   C5
Wellingtonbridge/
   Droichead Eoin   **30**   F7
Wells Cross   **10**   F4
Westport/*Cathair na Mart*   **14**   F4
Westport Quay   **13**   E4
Westtown   **35**   D2
Wexford/*Loch Garman*   **30**   H6
Wheelam Cr. Road   **23**   C4
White Gate Cross Roads   **32**   F1
White's Cross/
   Crois an Fhaoitigh   **33**   E4
Whiteabbey/*An Mhainistir Fhionn*   **10**   J1

Whitechurch/*An Teampall Geal*   **33**   E3
   Co Cork/*Corcaigh*
Whitechurch, Co Waterford   **34**   K2
Whitechurch, Co Wexford   **29**   E7
Whitecross/*Corr Leacht*   **9**   E6
Whitegate/*An Geata Bán*   **21**   C7
   Co Clare/*An Clár*
Whitegate/*An Geata Bán*   **34**   G5
   Co Cork/*Corcaigh*
Whitehall or Paulstown   **29**   D3
Whitehall/*An Baile Nua*   **16**   F5
   Co Roscommon/*Ros Comáin*
Whitehall, Co Westmeath   **16**   K6

Whitehead/*An Cionn Bán*   **4**   K7
Whites Town   **18**   H2
Whitesides Corner/
   An Phrochlais   **4**   F7
Wicklow/*Cill Mhantáin*   **24**   J6
Wilkinstown/*Baile Uilcín*   **17**   D5
Willbrook   **20**   H7
Williamstown/*Baile Liam*   **15**   B6
   Co Galway/*Gaillimh*
Williamstown/*Baile Liam*   **22**   F1
   Co Westmeath/*An Iarmhí*
Windgap/*Bearna na Gaoithe*   **29**   B5
Wolfhill/*Cnocán na Mactíre*   **23**   A7

Woodburn/*Sruth na Coille*   **10**   J1
Woodenbridge   **30**   J1
Woodford/*An Ghráig*   **21**   C5
Woodgreen   **4**   G7
Woodstown   **35**   E1

Yellow Furze   **17**   E5
Youghal/*Eochaill*   **34**   J4
   Co Cork/*Corcaigh*
Youghal, Co Tipperary   **21**   C7

Affiliated to the Golf Union of Ireland
This listing is by Province and County
The name of the Golf Club is preceded by the number of holes and followed by a page number, in bold type, and a map reference for the grid square in which the golf location symbol (⛳) appears.

CONNACHT

Co. GALWAY

18	Athenry	20 K3
18	Ballinasloe	21 D3
18	Connemara	19 A1
18	Galway	20 H3
9	Gort	20 K5
9	Loughrea	21 B4
9	Mountbellew	21 B1
18	Oughterard	20 G1
9	Portumna	21 D5
18	Tuam	14 K7

Co. LEITRIM

9	Ballinamore	16 G1
9	Carrick-on-Shannon	15 D2

Co. MAYO

9	Achill Island	13 B2
9	Ballina	14 H1
9	Ballinrobe	14 G6
9	Ballyhaunis	14 K4
9	Belmullet	5 B7
18	Castlebar	14 G4
9	Claremorris	14 J5
9	Mulranny	13 D3
9	Swinford	14 J3
18	Westport	13 E4

Co. ROSCOMMON

18	Athlone	22 F1
9	Ballaghaderreen	15 B3
9	Boyle	15 D2
9	Castlerea	15 B4
11	Roscommon	15 D6

Co. SLIGO

9	Ballymote	15 B1
18	Co. Sligo	7 B5
18	Enniscrone	6 H7
18	Strandhill	7 B6
9	Tubbercurry	15 A1

LEINSTER

Co. CARLOW

9	Borris	29 E4
18	Carlow	29 E1

Co. DUBLIN

18	Balbriggan	18 H6
18	Balcarrick	24 H1
18	Ballinascorney	24 F3
18	Beaverstown	18 H7
18	Beech Park	23 E3
18	Donabate	24 H1
18	Dun Laoghaire	24 H3
9	Finnstown	24 F2
18	Forrest Little	24 G1
18	Hermitage	24 F2
18	Hollywood Lakes	18 G7
18	The Island	24 H1
9	Killiney	24 H3
18	Kilternan	24 H3
18	Lucan	24 F2
27	Malahide	24 H1
18	Old Conna	24 H3
27	Portmarnock	24 H1
9	Rush	18 H7
18	Skerries	18 H7
18	Slade Valley	24 F3
18	Westmanstown	24 F2
18	Woodbrook	24 H3

DUBLIN CITY

9	Carrickmines	24 H3
18	Castle	24 G3
18	Clontarf	24 G2
27	Deer Park	24 H2
18	Edmonstown	24 G3
18	Elm Park	24 G3
9	Foxrock	24 H3
18	Grange	24 G3
10	Hazel Grove	24 F3
18	Howth	24 H2
18	Milltown	24 G3
18	Newlands	24 F3
18	Rathfarnham	24 G3
18	Royal Dublin	24 H2
18	St. Annes	24 H2

18	Stackstown	24 G3
9	Sutton	24 H2

Co. LAOIS

9	Abbeyleix	22 K7
18	Heath	23 A5
9	Mountrath	22 J6
18	Portarlington	23 A4
9	Rathdowney	28 K1

Co. KILDARE

9	Athy	23 C6
36	Bodenstown	23 D3
18	Castlewarden	23 E3
9	Cill Dara	23 C4
9	Clongowes	23 D2
18	Craddockstown	23 E4
18	Curragh	23 C4
18	Knockanally	23 D2
18	Naas	23 E3
18	K Club	23 E3
9	Woodlands	23 C3

Co. KILKENNY

9	Callan	29 B4
9	Castlecomer	29 C1
18	Kilkenny	29 C3
18	Mount Juliet	29 C4
18	Waterford	29 O7

Co. LONGFORD

18	Co. Longford	16 G5

Co. LOUTH

18	Ardee	17 E3
18	Co. Louth	18 G5
18	Dundalk	18 F2
18	Greenore	18 H1
9	Killinbeg	18 F2

Co. MEATH

27	Black Bush	17 E7
9	Gormanstown	18 G6
18	Headfort	17 C5
9	Kilcock	23 D1
18	Laytown & Bettystown	18 G5
27	Royal Tara	17 D6
18	Trim	17 C7

Co. OFFALY

18	Birr	22 F5
9	Edenderry	23 B2
18	Tullamore	22 J3

Co. WESTMEATH

18	Delvin	17 A6
9	Moate	22 G2
18	Mullingar	22 K1

Co. WEXFORD

18	Courtown	30 J3
18	Enniscorthy	30 G5
9	New Ross	29 D6
18	Rosslare	30 H7
18	Wexford	30 H6

Co. WICKLOW

18	Arklow	30 K1
9	Baltinglass	23 D7
18	Blainroe	24 J6
9	Bray	24 H4
18	Charlesland	24 J4
9	Coollattin	30 H2
18	Delgany	24 H4
18	The European	24 J7
18	Greystones	24 H4
9	Tulfarris	23 E5
18	Wicklow	24 J6
9	Woodenbridge	30 J1

MUNSTER

Co. CLARE

18	Dromoland	27 A1
18	Ennis	27 A1
9	Kilkee	26 F2

9	Kilrush	26 H3
36	Lahinch	20 F7
18	Shannon	27 A3
9	Spanish Point	26 H1

Co. CORK

18	Bandon	33 C6
9	Bantry Park	33 H6
9	Berehaven	32 F7
18	Charleville	27 C6
9	Cobh	34 G5
18	Cork	34 F4
9	Doneraile	33 D1
18	Douglas	34 F5
18	Dunmore	36 G5
18	East Cork	34 G4
18	Fermoy	34 F2
9	Frankfield	33 E5
18	Glengarrif	32 H6
9	Kanturk	33 B1
9	Kinsale	33 E6
9	Macroom	33 B4
18	Mahon	34 F4
18	Mallow	33 D2
27	Mitchelstown	27 E7
18	Monkstown	34 F5
18	Muskerry	33 D4
9	Raffeen Creek	34 F5
9	Skibbereen	35 E5
18	Youghal	34 K4
18	Harbour Point	34 F4

Co. KERRY

36	Ballybunion	26 F4
18	Ceann Sibeal	31 B1
18	Dooks	31 E2
9	Kenmare	32 H4
36	Killarney	32 H2
18	Parknasilla	32 F5
18	Tralee	25 E7
18	Waterville	31 C5
9	Castlegregory	25 D7

Co. LIMERICK

9	Adare Manor	27 B4
18	Castletroy	27 D3
9	Foynes	26 K3
18	Limerick	27 C3
9	Newcastle West	26 K5

Co. TIPPERARY

9	Cahir Park	28 H6
9	Carrick-on-Suir	29 B6
18	Clonmel	28 K6
18	Nenagh	29 E7
18	Rockwell	28 H5
18	Roscrea	22 G7
9	Templemore	28 J1
18	Thurles	28 J3
9	Tipperary	28 F5

Co. WATERFORD

9	Dungarvan	35 B2
9	Lismore	34 J2
18	Tramore	35 D1

ULSTER

Co. ANTRIM

18	Ballycastle	4 G2
18	Ballyclare	4 H7
18	Ballymena	4 G6
9	Bushfoot	3 E2
18	Cairndhu	4 J6
18	Carrickfergus	10 H1
9	Cushendall	4 H4
18	Greenisland	10 J1
9	Lambeg	10 H3
9	Larne	4 K6
18	Lisburn	10 H3
18	Massereene	10 G1
36	Rathmore	3 D2
36	Royal Portrush	3 D2
18	Whitehead	4 K7

Co. ARMAGH

18	Ashfield	17 E1
18	Co. Armagh	9 D5
18	Lurgan	10 F4

18	Portadown	10 F4
18	Silverwood	10 F4
18	Tandragee	10 F5

Co. CAVAN

9	Belturbet	16 J1
9	Blacklion	8 F6
9	Cabra Castle	17 D3
18	Co. Cavan	16 K2
18	Slieve Russell	8 H7
9	Virginia	17 B4

BELFAST

18	Balmoral	10 J2
18	Belvoir Park	10 J3
9	Cliftonville	10 J2
18	Dunmurry (New)	10 J3
18	Fortwilliam	10 J2
9	Gilnahirk	10 K2
18	Knock	10 K2
18	Knockbracken	10 J3
27	Malone	10 J3
9	Ormeau	10 J2
18	Shandon Park	10 J2

Co. LONDONDERRY

9	Brown Trout	3 D4
18	Castlerock	3 C3
18	City of Derry	2 K5
9	Kilrea	3 E5
18	Moyola	3 E7
18	Portstweart	3 D3

Co. FERMANAGH

18	Castlehume	8 H5
18	Enniskillen	8 H5

Co. MONAGHAN

9	Castleblayney	9 D7
9	Clones	8 K7
18	Nuremore	17 D2
9	Rossmore	9 B6

Co. TYRONE

18	Dungannon	9 C3
9	Fintona	8 K3
18	Killymoon Cookstown	9 D2
18	Newtownstewart	8 J1
18	Omagh	8 K2
18	Strabane	2 J7

Co. DONEGAL

18	Ballybofey & Stranolar	2 G7
18	Ballyliffin	2 J2
18	Buncrana	2 J3
18	Bundoran	7 D3
9	Cruit Island	1 C4
18	Donegal	7 E2
18	Dunfanaghy	2 F3
18	Greencastle	3 B2
9	Gweedore	1 D4
18	Letterkenny	2 G5
18	Narin & Portnoo	1 C7
18	North West	2 J4
9	Otway	2 H3
18	Portsalon	2 H3
9	Redcastle	3 A3
18	Rosapenna	2 G3

Co. DOWN

18	Ardglass	12 J6
18	Banbridge	11 E5
18	Bangor	12 J1
18	Bright Castle	12 H6
18	Carnalea	12 H1
18	Clandeboye	12 H2
18	Donaghadee	12 J1
18	Downpatrick	12 J5
9	Helens Bay	12 H1
18	Holywood	12 H2
9	Kilkeel	18 H1
18	Kirkistown Castle	12 K4
9	Mahee Island	12 J3
18	Mourne	12 G6
18	Royal County Down	12 G6
18	Royal Belfast	18 H1
18	Scrabo Newtownards	12 H2
18	Spa Ballinahinch	12 G4
18	Warrenpoint	18 G1